PROFIT HEROES

Endorsements

"Many of the buyers you encounter today are going to pressure you to reduce your price in order to win their business. Make no mistake, you are being commoditized. Without the business acumen to truly understand your client's business and justify the impact your solution has on your prospective client's profit, 'you are destined to compete on price.' Bob's recipe, if followed, is guaranteed to make you a profit hero--inside your client's company and your own."

—Anthony Iannarino is an entrepreneur, author, and speaker. He writes daily at www.iannarino.com

"I was reluctant to read another sales book. Then, a mutual friend of the author convinced me this was an important book. And he was right. Bob Rickert not only solves the puzzle of new buying behaviors, he provides a concrete methodology. *Profit Heroes* delivers a sales approach that meets 21st-century buyers' needs. You'll learn why buyers have changed, why their old strategies and tactics fail, what their new priorities are, new strategies that match these priorities, and how to develop a modern sales process that works. This is a must-have book for every sales organization."

—Gary Hart, CEO of SalesDuJour

"Warning: Everything you know about selling is wrong. Everything you have been taught before today is wrong. This book will upset you. You will have to relearn everything. You will have to learn about a new mindset: a profit mindset."

—Todd Schnick, CEO of Dreamland Media

"The needs of buyers are evolutionary. Salespeople need to *shuck and jive* with those changes or they will be left wondering why they are no longer successful. In *Profit Heroes*, Bob Rickert provides salespeople with the tools they need to stay at the top of their game. A must-read to succeed!"

—Lee B. Salz, bestselling author of *Hire Right, Higher Profits*

"Other sales books will tell you that you need to challenge your customers with fresh insights; *Profit Heroes* tells you *how*."

—Jack Malcolm, author of *Bottom-line Selling* and *Strategic Sales Presentations*

"With the dozens of new sales titles hitting the market each year, it's difficult for any of them to rise above. *Profit Heroes: Breakthrough Strategies for Winning Customers and Building Profits* is one of the rare exceptions that will get your attention, show you the light, show you how, and leave you with the knowledge needed to change the way you sell. Everyone knows the importance of selling value, but few can do it effectively. This book shows that selling profits dwarfs selling value in much the same way that high-speed broadband dwarfs dial-up. Don't just read this book; consume it, apply it, and outsell your competitors."

—Dave Kurlan, bestselling author of <u>Baseline Selling</u> and founder and CEO of Objective Management Group, Inc.

"Exceptional sales practices have always consisted of both art and science. *Profit Heroes* delves deeply into sales science as it has evolved since the Great Recession. It is both eye-opening and amazingly powerful. Don't just read it. Study it!"

—Tom Hopkins, author of *When Buyers Say No*

"Businesspeople tend to view the average salesperson in a negative way for a reason. For the most part, salespeople simply don't speak "business." They don't have an owner's or CEO's perspective on the day-to-day challenges of creating a profit. Instead, they approach a company with their own objectives in mind—to sell a product, hit a sales target, and earn a commission or bonus. Bob Rickert's new book, *Profit Heroes,* is a bright-light addition to the sales profession! Using a business novel approach (think Patrick Lencioni), Bob shares the secrets of how big-time sales are made when a salesperson effectively understands and addresses the core financial issues of a company. Much more than simply an «ROI» message, *Profit Heroes* details how truly connecting a product or service to a customer›s profitability can turn an average salesperson into a sales superstar! You, too, can become a *Profit Hero*!"

—Kelly Riggs, author, speaker, performance coach; one of "50 Sales Pros to Follow on Twitter"; host of "The Business LockerRoom"

"Now, more than ever, salespeople need to understand finance and profitability if they are to sell effectively to the C-suite. Fortunately, Bob Rickert has written an informative and thoroughly enjoyable book that provides a roadmap for salespeople seeking to become "Profit Heroes." Using realistic examples, Bob paints a picture of how to sell successfully using executive board language, and contrasts it with the unsuccessful strategy of a firm that takes a different approach. The information Bob provides is so powerful that I would like to include it in a course for our sales students at K-State! I highly recommend this book to anyone in the sales arena."

—Dr. Dawn Deeter-Schmelz, professor; director of the National Strategic Selling Institute; and J. J. Vanier Distinguished Chair of Relational Selling & Marketing, Kansas State University

"Sometimes the most obvious is often ignored. Bob uncovers what other experts have ignored in this dynamic business book, *Profit Heroes.* He takes you by the hand and shows you how to craft a path toward sustainable and even transformational business growth."

—Leanne Hoagland-Smith, CRO & H2H Heurist for ADVANCED
SYSTEMS

"Sales success in the 21st century requires salespeople to engage customers in terms relevant to them. This means focusing on business results, their performance improvement, and ultimately, on their improved profitability. *Profit Heroes* is a pragmatic guide to helping sales professionals speak their customers' language, engaging them in discussions about business outcomes. If you aren't having these discussions, then you aren't creating value for your customers. If you aren't talking customer profitability, then, as Bob illustrates, you are likely to lose to a competitor who is."

—Dave Brock, Partners In EXCELLENCE

"It's one thing to say salespeople should make the economic case for their proposal. It's quite another to describe in detail just what that means, how it should be done, and how to embed that approach in your sales organization. That's what Bob Rickert does in his book *Profit Heroes*, and he does it well and with rich examples."

—Charles H. Green, Trusted Advisor Associates

"The first two chapters are absolutely riveting. You read about a salesperson who lost the sale and was devastated. You read about the salesperson who won the sale and was elated. Anyone who has sold has felt both of these emotions. But Bob Rickert makes those emotions palpable. Once he hooks you emotionally, he provides the roadmap for winning more and bigger deals. If you want to be seen as a peer—a businessperson who happens to sell—instead of "just another salesperson," *Profit Heroes* belongs at the top of your must-read list."

—Chris Lytle, author of *The Accidental Salesperson*

"So many sellers fumble around when it comes to building and communicating the return-on-investment case. Those that do it well win the most sales. Sellers who want to do it well would be wise to read *Profit Heroes*. Twice."

—Mike Schultz, bestselling author of *Insight Selling: Surprising Research on What Sales Winners Do Differently*

"*Profit Heroes* is a must-read for any salesperson or manager who is selling complex, high-ticket solutions. In his book, Bob Rickert presents one of the most accurate and detailed depictions that I have ever read of the steps a sophisticated salesperson must go through to compete for and win a large deal. That alone is worth the price of the book. However, Bob also provides an extremely useful tutorial on financial literacy for salespeople. Salespeople today have to possess a higher level of business acumen to help their customers make the most profitable purchase decisions, and *Profit Heroes* shows them how to read and mine their customer's financial statements for data that will help them formulate solutions that will win deals."

—Andy Paul, author of *Zero-Time Selling: 10 Essential Steps to Accelerate Every Company's Sales*

"Modern buyers are empowered, finicky, and demanding. They expect more from sellers than ever before, and smart sellers deliver more. More what? Well, as Bob Rickert has astutely identified in *Profit Heroes*, the sellers who win today are the ones who deliver more value by driving more profit for their buyers. These savvy sellers have the business acumen to strategize and articulate exactly how they will drive profit. In doing so, they connect with buyers in meaningful and lasting ways. You, too, can become a profit hero thanks to Bob's carefully crafted how-to-manual and stories in *Profit Heroes*."

—Deb Calvert, author of *DISCOVER Questions™ Get You Connected*

"Bob's focus on 'profit' could not be more on-target. In a recent dialogue with industry CEOs, there was 'table-pounding' agreement that all employees, including sales, marketing, finance, operations, HR, and IT, must all know how they impact profit improvement."

—Dr. Douglas A. Fisher, assistant professor and director of the Center for Supply Chain Management, Marquette University

"*Profit Heroes* describes how sales losers can become sales winners, even in a rapidly changing business world."

—Geoffrey James, author of *Business Without the Bullsh*t*

"Bob Rickert's book turns the sales game on its head. It is about winning and losing and how the challenger won against the incumbent. The salesperson turned an opportunity into a financial decision rather than a technical one, because she knew that profit trumps price every day of the week. Learn how to talk profit. Get your copy of *Profit Heroes*."

—Joanne Black, author of *No More Cold Calling: The Breakthrough System That Will Leave Your Competition in the Dust*

"I love Bob Rickert's *Profit Heroes* because he beautifully articulates a message everyone in sales need to hear: You can't win as a sales professional by competing on price. And then Rickert shows us how to understand "customer profitability" in a succinct and compelling way so we can sell value and differentiate ourselves from the competition. Please read this book and stop whining that all the customer cares about is price!"

—Mike Weinberg, author of the Amazon #1 bestseller *New Sales. Simplified*, and CEO of The New Sales Coach consultancy

"This book doesn't only contain a great story of all three views of a deal (the winner, the loser, the customer); it also lays out the steps you can take to do all of the things the winner did in your next deal…and beyond. In today's marketplace your prospects don't need a salesperson to tell them about products, services, or solutions—they can find all that information online for themselves. What today's buyers need is a salesperson who understand BUSINESS. Helping your prospects tie everything they do (or want to do) to the profitability of their company is the way to get them off their status quo and doing something…plus that something will be with you."

—Lynn Hidy, founder of UpYourTelesales.com

"Far beyond most b2b sales books released these days, this is a detailed examination of the new way to look at the sales process based on financial impact and profits created for customers, rather than simply product and services delivered. The result is not just for salespeople and sales managers who are navigating the waters of creating value, competing on price, and trying to differentiate. It is a book for every level of company leadership, and one that can truly prepare any business for the future of selling."

—Andrea Waltz, co-author of *Go for Go!*

"At the end of the day, virtually all companies exist solely to make money for their owners. In Bob Rickert's book *Profit Heroes: Breakthrough Strategies for Winning Customers and Building Profits*, his approach to selling profit improvement is spot on. I enjoyed the winner and loser stories. Well done. His deep dive into the techniques and use of resources is extremely helpful to anyone doing strategic selling. Wonderful book!!"

—Tom VanHootegem, retired sales executive

"Bob Rickert has advanced how the sales cycle should be conducted for sales and businesspeople to experience excellent success. It is a brilliant and an up-to-date guide for readers to adjust to the new way of conducting sales. The tagline of his book, *The Profit Heroes*, says it all: *Breakthroughs Strategies for Winning Customers and Building Profits.*"

—Elinor Stutz, CEO, Inspirational Speaker and Author Smooth Sale

PROFIT HEROES

Breakthrough Strategies for Winning
Customers and Building Profits

Bob Rickert

authorHOUSE®

AuthorHouse™ LLC
1663 Liberty Drive
Bloomington, IN 47403
www.authorhouse.com
Phone: 1-800-839-8640

Published by AuthorHouse   08/04/2014

ISBN: 978-1-4918-4662-9 (sc)
ISBN: 978-1-4918-4636-0 (hc)
ISBN: 978-1-4918-4661-2 (e)

Library of Congress Control Number: 2013923251

Any people depicted in stock imagery provided by Thinkstock are models, and such images are being used for illustrative purposes only. Certain stock imagery © Thinkstock.

This book is printed on acid-free paper.

Contents

Foreword

DAN WALDSCHMIDT

Ultra-runner, and bestselling author of *EDGY Conversations: How Ordinary People Can Achieve Outrageous Success*

All of life is a soap opera of profit and loss. Right? You win big. You lose big. There's drama around every corner.

Business is a big part of that drama. Yet how often have you read a business book—better yet a sales or marketing book—that tells you how to do a better job at growing profitable revenue?

And that's where you need help the most.

There has always seemed to be a natural tension between the bean counters in the back office who wear green visors and ask that expenses be stapled to the correct form, and the red-blooded, meat-eating sales executives who woo clients and attract the next generation of clientele.

The sales team always feel as if they have their hands tied behind their back. The finance guys wonder if the sales team ever took basic arithmetic.

I know. I've been there.

The first company that I grew by millions of dollars was a huge learning experience managing profitability. I was brought in to do a turnaround and thought that meant that we were going to do a complete aim-for-the-fences turnaround. Dramatic change was going to happen.

Boy was I fooled. To me it seemed as if the owners wanted more revenue, but they weren't willing to make the dramatic investment that creating lots of new revenue required. Despite those challenges, we grew more than a 1,000% in less than two years—and over the next few years to more than $100 million in annual revenue.

In my next venture I took a technology company on a wild ride of revenue growth, catapulting overall sales again by more than 1,000% in the first year alone. That's when I begin to notice all the problems. We couldn't fulfill all the orders that we were taking in.

Obviously somebody was lazy. Obviously the team wasn't working hard enough. In my mind we needed a whole new management team. I was out the door, headed to the next wild adventure on my business roadmap.

Then something awful happened and I was forced to learn the importance of managing profitability: I was offered the CEO job of that technology company I had grown so fast.

The majority shareholders asked me if I would consider running the company instead of leaving it. "You can do whatever you want; just go make us some money." I still remember the conversation.

I was going to show these idiots how to run a company. That's when I began to realize how much of an idiot *I* was. I had no clue what "profitable revenue" really was. I knew what profit was and how to sell, but I didn't understand the connection between the two.

I learned fast. I had to. When you're in the driver's seat of a runaway train you either slam on the brakes or try to steer your way clear of danger and finish the trip successfully. I decided to get some help.

I brought in a strong team to help me figure it out. Five years later the company was purchased and I was on to the next thing. But the lessons I learned about how to sell profitably have stayed with me.

I had to learn these lessons the hard way—right in the middle of the boiler room. It was hot and messy. And there were casualties everywhere. Most of those were my own doing, unfortunately.

I hope you can save yourself from similar nonsense by reading this book and learning the lessons you'll find inside. It'll make you a better business leader, a better sales executive, a better salesperson, and a better overall person. Go be awesome.

To Andrea, Thank you for your unwavering love and support, and for encouraging me to write about my passion.

To Audrey and Nick, I am inspired by you every day of my life. Thank you for pursuing your dreams and striving to achieve your endless potential. I am incredibly proud of you.

Introduction

The Need to Transform Selling

I wrote this book because I believe selling is undergoing its most significant change in more than 30 years. For those who recognize it, there is a "call to arms" that is transforming how sellers must sell and what it will take to succeed in the future. Those who don't recognize it, or fail to heed it, will be left clinging to outdated assumptions and miscalculations about the centers of influence and the new business metrics that are fast becoming the primary currency in every customer exchange.

In the past, recessions and significant market shifts occurred gradually, over a period of years. They were typically observable and predictable, and executive leaders had time to evolve new strategies as market conditions were reshaped.

But things are different today. The financial meltdown, the Great Recession, the anemic recovery, and stubbornly high jobless rates, as well as uncertainty about healthcare reform, tax policy, energy policy, and immigration, conspire to change how customers *think*, *behave*, and *manage* their business. We are now told that this is the "new normal."

To thrive in the future, salespeople must understand how customers are changing and what it will take to win in the new economy. It is no longer about your company against mine, or your products and services against mine, or your know-how against mine. Now it is all about profitability and the ability to identify it, quantify it, sell it, and deliver it. To win today you must be viewed by customers as more than "a vendor." You must now become "an earnings contributor."

Customer Behavior

We are seeing this trend play out in how customers are behaving. Customers are demanding a financial return on every investment they make—not just anecdotal evidence, but actual, documented, hard-dollar impact. They expect you to know and articulate specifically how your solution will affect their ability to grow their business or better manage their cost structure. They are managing their capital and their cash flow by demanding longer payment terms, which puts added pressure on your company. You may have customers like some of the largest U.S. corporations that are muscling their suppliers into 120-day terms on receivables. Four months to get paid! That means for suppliers to win and keep customers, they have to absorb a huge hit to their own cash flow just to stay in the game.

More than ever before, customers know that every dollar of price you or your competitors give away improves the customer's operating income. That's why procurement departments are given financial incentives to take money out of your pocket; it strengthens the financial performance of their companies. In today's chaotic economy, desperate competitors who are unable to build a case for their economic impact further contribute to the downward spiral of price and margin compression. The selling game has changed, and its new language is *profitability*.

A New Kind of Risk Management

As I write this in 2014, we're five years and counting into the economic recovery, but despite rising corporate profits and new highs for stock values, it still feels as if we are in the middle of a recession. This dichotomy directly reflects a new kind of corporate risk management. At every level of the company, executives have put greater rigor and discipline into financial management in order to avoid a repeat of 2008 and 2009.

The risk of unforeseen external events, unpredictable revenue growth, or another round of capital shortages like we experienced in 2009 are all forcing a stricter adherence to budgets than ever before. In a growth environment, funding is easier to access, budgets are more robust, and there is money available to move from one initiative to another when priorities change. But today, if the need arises for an additional investment that wasn't budgeted, good luck getting the mind share, let alone the approval of senior management. Risk aversion and caution are overriding the risk taking and "pushing the envelope" that we saw in growth environments.

To get decision makers and influencers at any level to take a risk in this environment is a big hurdle. For salespeople it means understanding that executive management expects every decision to be made with three principles in mind. First, how will your solution help us drive top-line growth? Second, how will your solution help us manage our costs more effectively? And third, if you are asking for capital, how will it be utilized to either grow the business or make us more efficient? Selling to an economic decision maker today requires thinking like one and ultimately behaving like one.

Profit-Centered Selling

Looking back at the evolution of selling over the past 30 years, early on it was about product, price, and availability. Next, when sellers discovered that competing on product features and price didn't help them win, they began to redefine their approach in terms of what became known as "solution selling." That worked for a while as bundling products, services, know-how, and problem solving into a differentiated approach helped defuse the power of price in the decision. Today, the prominent sales strategy is "value selling," but if salespeople don't have a clear way to define the profitability that they can deliver, most are left to compete at the wrong levels with the wrong message—and too often reap the wrong outcome.

A New Mindset

The core of the new sales transformation is a new mindset, a different way of thinking about what you sell and how you sell. When I ask salespeople what it is that they sell, most define their solutions in operational terms. They are quick to describe their products or service capabilities and their well-oiled value proposition, which includes things like speed, quality, service, operational efficiencies, and even tangible dollar savings. Yet at the moment of truth they usually end up comparing their solution with their competitors', and the difference they point to is usually cost.

The fact is, all successful organizations have invested heavily in their products and services, their know-how, and their service model. They all bring tremendous value in the form of customer profit improvement every single day. It might be the high-end window manufacturer that builds a bar coding system into its product identification to help building contractors match blueprints with an individual window, thus eliminating the costly repair or replacement of windows that leak and cause customer complaints. Or it could be a jet engine manufacturer that has created engineering efficiencies that drive down fuel costs, lower noise levels, and improve emissions to address corporate and governmental standards. But the question is, do their customers understand the impact to their bottom line?

Too often they do not, and as a consequence, the companies are not rewarded for the financial impact they deliver. I continually hear from sales leadership that salespeople concede too quickly on price or give away time, effort, expertise, and resources without a value exchange in spite of the fact that tangible financial impact was delivered. Why? Because most view their relationship with the customer in terms of what they are selling and not the financial impact of what they are delivering. It is up to the salespeople to know how to identify, quantify, and communicate their financial impact. If they don't, who will? We know customers won't do it. If you are unaware of how much economic impact you deliver, you will fall victim to the only metric left that customers do understand: *price*. Let's face it, price is quantifiable.

Who Are the Profit Heroes?

Profit Heroes are a new breed of salesperson. To their customers, they are more than partners; they are viewed as peers. Profit Heroes know how to speak the language of finance and profitability, and they understand how customers make economic decisions. They bring ideas, thought leadership, and innovation to every interaction. They know their customers better than their competitors. They know how to analyze the customer's business and offer profit-centered solutions that achieve results. They understand how to identify, quantify, and sell profit impact. And they can prove it.

So when customers ask a Profit Hero, "What do you sell?" the answer is always the same and it's resounding: *I sell and deliver profit improvement!* This book is intended to help you achieve your own transformation to Profit Hero.

A Competition

Selling is an emotional profession. You lose more than you win, so you are always dealing with rejection, always in a relentless battle to acquire new customers while retaining the ones you have. Aggressive competitors are constantly vying for your customers, and events you can't control can change your fortunes in a minute. Yet we do it because there is nothing more fulfilling than winning business for your company, where so many people rely on you. Celebrating with a committed team that rejoices in every win is exhilarating. But most of all, it is the thrill of the race, the personal challenge to be better and to achieve greatness in a profession that holds their "rainmakers" in high esteem.

I open this book with a story about two competing rainmakers. This unique inside and emotional view of two competing salespeople who faced off in the pursuit of a very important opportunity illustrates today's transformation in the world of sales. Both of these salespeople represent great companies who have fine products and provide good service. Both are highly talented and successful—motivated and driven to learn and succeed. And they work for leadership that invests in them and their success. Theirs is a classic competition you see every day in American business, and is what makes selling the most exciting profession in the world.

The two competitors' stories of winning and losing make up the first two chapters of this book. They are a compilation of real and fictional events. I use the salespeople's experiences in the rest of the book to illustrate my strategies for becoming a Profit Hero, and to demonstrate how companies can build a culture of competing on profit. You may have had experiences like theirs; I know I have.

The remainder of the book unveils the strategies and approaches that Profit Heroes use to achieve success. I outline the "profit-centered sales process" and provide the concepts and tools used by the winning salesperson, Susan Stafford, to win the biggest deal of her career! These strategies are proven and will assist you in becoming a Profit Hero. I describe Stafford's thought processes at key intervals, as well as the viewpoints of the customer's executives and her own team.

Chapter 1

Autopsy of a Lost Sale—
The Loser's View

"Most of our assumptions have outlived their usefulness."
—Marshall McLuhan

This is a fictional representation of two companies involved in a large opportunity and how the winning and losing salespeople dealt with the challenges of competing for the business. National Products is the customer. The company manufactures sinks, tubs, washing systems, and many other products for residential and commercial construction and industrial applications. They sell direct, through distribution, and a large part of their business is done through do-it-yourself "big-box" retailers.

National Products embarked on a quality improvement audit of its manufacturing facilities to address product quality problems, defects, and refinishing problems resulting from outdated spray gun equipment as well as other system-related factors. This is the inside story of how two strong competitors, Quality Brands (and account manager Vince Billings) and High Beam Industries (and account manager Susan Stafford), vied for a large project to upgrade the manufacturing process at National Products.

At Quality Brands

The following is an exchange between two Quality Brands executives: Executive Vice President of Sales Lamar Johnson and CEO Jim Thomas.

Lamar: I am sorry to report that we were informed today by National Products that they have awarded their large quality improvement project to High Beam Industries. We are really disappointed and frankly shocked. All of our key contacts, a number of whom we have worked closely with for the past five years, all seemed to be caught off guard by this decision.

Jim: That is very disappointing. We were all counting on this revenue—I believe it was worth over $5 million; is that correct? I understand that we were very aggressive in pricing this deal and that we put a lot of resources on it to ensure we were positioned for success. Why did we lose?

Lamar: We're trying to get more information. The account manager Vince Billings and I are going to meet with the CFO and the head of manufacturing on Friday to discuss their decision and to see if we can persuade them to reconsider.

Jim: What's your hunch?

Lamar: Well first, the scope seemed to change late in the game and we were unable to fully respond in time. They gave us specific parameters for their new spray gun systems upgrade, but then changed them at the last minute. So, I think I can use that as leverage. I know this is a big disappointment for us, but I can assure you that we put everything we had into this and felt very strongly that our proposal was spot-on and stronger than High Beam's.

Jim: I would like to understand the reasons why we lost. We need to make sure we evaluate how

> **au•top•sy**—*Examination of a sales process to determine or confirm the cause of death. Also called postmortem examination, a critical assessment after the fact*

we're approaching customers and deals of this size. I want to make certain we've considered all of the factors that will drive our future success. Please provide me these kinds of details after your debrief. I want your sales leadership team to do an autopsy on this deal so we don't encounter this again in the future.

I hope you are able to turn this around. Let us know what we can do from the executive level.

Vince Billings says:
My View on Losing the Business

This was a crushing defeat. I believed, and still do to this day, that we were the better choice, that we have better-performing products. I know that we had long provided better service in the form of problem solving and quality improvement. For example, earlier this year when National Products' paint mixtures were off and quality suffered, we brought in a technical specialist who helped them calibrate their systems, which resolved the problem quickly. I know that alone saved them a lot of money. But not only that, with the relationships I've developed over the past five years, frankly I was just shocked. I didn't see this one coming.

My Relationships with National Products

I have been managing this account for five years. When I started, it was a less-than-half-million-dollar-a-year revenue account with very low margins. In fact, that is why they gave it to me. I have a track record of taking underperforming accounts and turning them around. I have made sales quota each of the past seven years, three times as top seller, once as runner-up. Always in the top 10 out of 200 salespeople.

When I took over this account, my vice president of sales, Pat Farris, acknowledged that things hadn't gone well in the past. He felt there was the potential to generate at least $3 million in annual revenue based on National Products' global growth, our lack of penetration into the account, and three new products in our portfolio to strengthen our position and give us a competitive advantage.

Early on, when I took over this account, I discovered that our relationships were only at the procurement level. My predecessor had not done much to elevate within the organization. In his defense, six years ago we had some major quality issues that almost certainly affected the relationship with National. Nonetheless, when I got there I didn't have much to work with. Overall, as the largest player in the industry, we only had about 10% of their spray gun systems business, while the rest went to three other companies.

The first thing I did was to understand our history. I wanted to see if there were any buried skeletons that I needed to know about. Then I dug into how they were organized, where their facilities were, and what type of manufacturing they were doing at each location so I could diagnose where we could add value with our products. Our product engineering and support services are absolutely world class in our industry, as evidenced by our Quality Product Awards and recognition from the key manufacturing associations that track and measure quality management outcomes.

The good news is that I built this account to $2.5 million a year. That's by basically winning every opportunity that National Products put out for proposal. In addition to the guns and systems we installed, I sold National a monitoring system that helped them manage their production paint quality. With the relationships I've built and by leveraging our engineering resources, I've been able to show them tremendous operational efficiencies that I know have saved them millions.

The National Products Company Initiative

One of the National people I work closely with on day-in and day-out is Chet Gretzky, director of manufacturing operations. He sits two levels down from Executive Vice President of Manufacturing Rich Bacus and is the go-to guy on the manufacturing side of the business because of his long tenure and performance over the years. He has the ear of senior management and survives, in fact flourishes, every time there is executive turnover.

Chet called me up in early June with a heads-up that there had been an operations meeting about production quality and outcomes. The meeting included a review of an internal audit to identify process improvement areas that could support the company's business goals.

He said that, of the 42 plants National Products operates worldwide, at least 20 needed updating in their paint application processes, including replacing their spray gun systems and pumps, plus better information for improved operational decision support. Evidently they want at least 20 spray gun systems, with pumps, design engineering, installation services, monitoring equipment, and more. Chet said they were expecting to invest about $200,000 to $250,000 per assembly line, or between $4 million and $5 million in total to bring them up to date with the latest technology and to ensure they hit their throughput benchmarks. This made sense. Older spray guns can clog, and operational wear and tear means more downtime for repairs and maintenance. Parts are getting harder to find and they are expensive. Older equipment is less energy-efficient—a big factor with the rising cost of energy. But most of all, they can get better-quality outcomes at a lower cost with new guns that can handle higher pressures over sustained periods.

Chet said that he would have more details within the week and would provide as much information as he could. At that point he didn't know whether they would put this out for RFP or identify a short list of companies that they believe would be capable of delivering a project of this size, but he committed to getting an answer to that as soon as he could.

My Internal Discussions

This deal was huge. In fact, this would have been the single biggest deal I ever sold. Up to now my biggest was a $2 million agreement that rolled out over three years. This would have been up to $5 million! I called Pat right away to let him know that this project might have serious legs. I had been hearing rumblings from the plant managers and production managers about paint application quality causing real problems, like line shutdowns for maintenance and repairs because the spray guns were faulting and clogging. They often had to send product down for repaint and touch-up before they could ship. But I never knew it was as big a problem as they discovered in their audit. All I knew was, I will take it. Hey, after all the other deals I chase at other companies that don't happen, I deserve a deal like this.

Pat suggested that we get a team meeting together to include Lily Chang, who heads up Product Development, our manufacturing team to make sure we could get the products manufactured in time, and our installation services team so they could put a large installation plan into their workflow. And of course we needed someone from Finance for the internal and sales pricing data that will become part of our proposal. All hands on deck, we need this one.

Beforehand, Pat asked me to prepare an initial strategy for this opportunity, including a review of National Products' financials, how they are organized, who we know, where we have influence, our installed product, and the customer's level of satisfaction. He also wanted to know any history that would help or hurt our chances.

My One-on-One with Pat Farris

Here's what I reported back to Pat. While profitable, National Products had seen revenue flatten out, gross margins were down, and operating profit was below expectations. I suspect that coming in below expectations is one of the reasons they were looking for areas where they could improve.

I explained that I had worked hard to build relationships as high up in the organization as possible, and especially at the production and manufacturing levels. Nothing gets purchased if the production team isn't asking for it or supporting it. This is how I've been able to avoid doing everything through procurement. While I still sometimes get beat up on price, I am able to get help from their production team, plant managers, and others in requesting our products and with key production metrics that justify our higher prices. It has worked well.

Pat asked me who would be making this decision. From what I understood, it would be EVP of Manufacturing Rich Bacus, VP of Manufacturing Lester Powers, Manufacturing Finance Director Aisha Henderson, production leaders with a couple of key plant managers contributing, and one or two others who are closest to the production facilities and their quality issues. He asked me about the executives and the role they might play in this. He felt we needed to cover our bases to ensure we get to them along the way.

He suggested that I pull down all of the key executives' LinkedIn profiles, hit their website for executive bios, executive presentations, and press releases, as well as Google them for anything that might pop up (articles or mentions in *Forbes, Wall Street Journal*)—anything that could provide us insight and leverage. He especially wanted me to look into the LinkedIn connections so we could see their backgrounds, whether they had spent time at other Quality Brands customers, and if they are connected to anyone who could assist us. I told him I know the CFO and that he has been in a number of meetings I was a part of.

He knows us well and the service we provide and has been very supportive. I began my research.

My Next Steps

Knowing that this project grew out of National Products' production quality internal audit, Pat suggested that we request a copy of the audit so we could familiarize ourselves with the findings. It would be important to have that for the internal team meeting to get everyone's perspective on the best way to approach this opportunity and to win the business.

As I expected, Pat wanted to know who we are up against for this project. He knows our competitors well, and there are some we match up well with and others we might have a challenge with, basically price-driven companies that always make our lives difficult.

Finally, Pat asked me what my strategy was for winning this business. I told him that it was early but I believed that we had a strong position in the account now with the people who have the most influence on this decision in terms of the technical requirements and what is needed. And I outlined my initial strategy for him.

My Initial Strategy

There were three elements to my initial strategy for this opportunity. First, I needed to document all of the value we had delivered to National Products over the past five years. That would include all of the ways we had solved problems, saved them money, and kept their assembly lines running. I also wanted to get some of their performance metrics on throughput, where I know we've had some measurable results. We have delivered so much value, and this is our opportunity to remind them and get credit for it at the most important time in the relationship. I believed we would be the higher-priced solution and didn't want to get into a price battle, so these metrics would be useful in defending our price.

Second, we needed to demonstrate the benefits of going with Quality Brands because of the ease of integrating the new systems with National Products' existing spray gun systems. We would be a lower-cost and more efficient answer because of things like seamless installation and shorter ramp time for operator training and support. We needed to build a strong story here to make this seem like a very logical and easy decision.

Third, I had learned over time that National Products' CEO and CFO had high confidence in the judgment of their production leadership team, where we have such great relationships, so I planned to leverage them for two main things: getting as much information as possible that would help us shape the solution that would favor us over our competitors, and managing the buying process all the way to closing. Clearly, I wanted to get to the CFO and CEO if I could. But I also felt the need to dance with those who brought me to the party. I needed to take their lead at this point, and to be careful I didn't upset the apple cart politically. In my heart, I believed this was our deal to lose. Getting to the CEO or CFO would be tricky.

National Products' Project Description and Request for Information (RFI)

I got an email from National Products with an RFI from procurement. In my view, sending out an RFI is a way to appear open to all potential suppliers; yet at the same time it is a way to pare the list down to a manageable number.

An RFI is primarily used to gather information to help make a decision about what steps to take next. RFIs are typically not the final stage and are instead often used in combination with a request for proposal (RFP). I called Chet and he confirmed the scope of the project. It was in fact as big as I had hoped. He said the scope of National Products' Production Quality Improvement Initiative included the following:

Project Goals
1. Increase product throughput by 5%
2. Reduce defects and/or re-finishing rates by 5%
3. Reduce production downtime due to maintenance and repairs by 10%
4. Improve energy efficiency to meet corporate sustainability goals
5. Improve maintenance monitoring and reporting

Project Specifications
- 20 plants with 1 assembly line each = 20 lines
- 1 spray gun system (spray booths, pumps, hoses, canisters, cleaning sinks, gun racks, and other accessories) per line
- Installation services (including engineering designs, change-over services)
- Maintenance management software for facility-specific equipment performance monitoring
- Ongoing equipment servicing program for parts and repair services
- All systems to be installed and operational by March 31 to correspond with the beginning of the second-quarter production cycle
- Decision to be made no later than October 31

I asked Chet if I could get a copy of the production quality internal audit that was done on the production system so that I could get a sense of what they had found and where the shortcomings were, as well as learn more about the metrics that they were looking to improve. This would provide the baseline I used to link my value to their needs. The audit wasn't for public consumption, but I was able to get Chet to let me have it so that I could begin formulating my strategy for the proposal.

When I got the audit, I immediately asked my product development manager, Lily Chang, to help me think through all of the requirements we should anticipate and to start formulating our approach based on National Products' stated goals. I wanted her input before the internal team meeting so I could guide our conversation and make sure all the team members were up to speed.

Lily pointed out that in order to quantify the operational performance they were trying to improve, we needed specific production numbers, such as: assembly line downtime for maintenance, amount of labor hours that are going into the repair or replacement of equipment (guns, pumps, hoses, etc.), data on energy costs, and more.

I also wanted to know current throughput numbers in the targeted plants and what they hoped to achieve with the new equipment. We have such a strong track record of documenting higher levels of performance in product throughput, and I knew this was a critical metric to any manufacturing environment, so I saw this as a centerpiece of our differentiation and a competitive advantage.

The Proposal Review Process

I asked Chet if they were planning to put out an RFP following the RFI, and/or whether in this case they would create a short list of companies they would invite to submit a proposal. I was ready for either, but obviously I preferred the short list of competitors we know, because then we could position our solution against their weaknesses.

Chet is a big fan of ours and always supports Quality Brands when it comes down to us versus a competitor. His help has also been valuable with procurement when it comes time to quote a price for POs. I mean, I love Chet. He is a National Products lifer, started right out of high school and worked his way up the ranks. He earned a college degree in manufacturing engineering technologies over the years at night. He's been a valuable employee for them, and he's really well regarded there.

The procurement people were pushing for an RFP for an expenditure this big, but Chet and his team were able to steer them away from it. I like to think I influenced that as I went out to several of my contacts at National Products, including manufacturing leads, line supervisors, and plant managers (at least five of the 20 that were targeted for retrofitting) and convinced them that putting out an RFP would be an expensive distraction because of their unique requirements and the familiarity with their company that the project would require. Of course, selfishly, I knew that I had the inside track, because I would be able to base our solution on the depth of our relationship, the significance of what we had installed to date, and our excellent service record.

So, the good news was that this would be a competition without the heavy hand of procurement. It would be left to the experts to ensure they found the right solution for their production requirements.

The Competition

I didn't hear anything from National Products for two weeks about how they were going to be making this decision and who the competitors would be. Then I was informed in early August that they had narrowed the field down from six companies to just two, Quality Brands and High Beam Industries. I was a little surprised that they had eliminated so many companies so early, and I was even more surprised that it was High Beam Industries that had made the final cut. There were three other companies that had 30% of National Products' business, we had 60%, and High Beam had 10% or less.

High Beam had really been out of the picture for a while. The perception in the market was that they were not as innovative and didn't have the breadth and depth we did. Plus, frankly, I think their products are inferior, and that's not just me the sales guy talking; I have heard that from other customers. Either way, I felt good about going up against only High Beam, because in my opinion two of the excluded companies were stronger contenders for this business. They have competitive products and strong histories with National.

I knew that High Beam had not been in National much in the past couple of years, although I did hear that they had a new account manager and that she was making attempts to get into the account. Chet mentioned that she had contacted Rich Bacus, but he hadn't heard about any outcome. Didn't sound alarming, but you never know. One thing I knew for sure, she did not have the relationships or the history I do, and those take time to develop.

The Decision-Making Process

It wasn't clear to me yet what approach National Products was going to take in evaluating the two companies, and who and how the final decision would be made, but I was bent on making sure I influenced every aspect of it that I could. At first I heard that proposals would be submitted, manufacturing would make a recommendation to the executive committee, and they would pretty much take their advice and rubber stamp it. That was my working assumption throughout the early stages of the selling process. That is how it had worked numerous times in the past, even with large purchases. This was coming firsthand from the team that was in place to evaluate the companies and their solutions and that was responsible for making the recommendation. Can you say "driver's seat"? But I said to myself, don't rest on your laurels; time to get to work.

My Sales Process

Not that I didn't realize what a big deal this was, but Pat told me it could make the year for the company! He said it was on the radar of our CEO and CFO and they wanted to make sure we did everything possible to win this business. Any resources I needed I would be able to get. Of course, that was added pressure, but I felt confident because of our advantages at National: my relationships, our installations, and our service record.

Still, you can't take anything for granted, and there is always a risk that something weird or unexpected will happen. As a salesperson I have always hesitated to forecast something this big. When this large an opportunity is on our executives' radar, every day is a day of "informing" the leadership team of our progress. Oh well, it comes with the territory. I was more confident about this one because this National Products initiative was in our wheelhouse. It was what we do best!

As for my sales process, I believed my first step needed to be working with National's production team to analyze their business, confirm, the specs and goals of the project, and fully leverage their influence on the decision. Getting to the CEO and CFO was also a major objective to ensure that they knew about the relationship we had established and the performance we had delivered. I knew I needed to handle that diplomatically, since my relationships were with production. I also knew we needed to deliver a powerful presentation that would overwhelm them with the benefits of working with Quality Brands.

As for the approach my competitor might be using, I tried to get my contacts to give me some "intel" on what they were hearing, but I didn't get much on that. Knowing what I did about High Beam, my feeling was that they might try to sell on price, given our level of account penetration. In short, they might try to buy the business.

The Quality Brands Team Project Planning Meeting

It was my job to bring the team up to speed on National Products and our currently installed equipment, and to review National's Production Quality Improvement Initiative. In the meeting, in addition to Pat Farris and Lily Chang, I had Bill Bankowski, the installation director; Jason Miller, who leads the technical sales support organization; and Joyce Simmons from the finance group, who works closely with sales, pricing, and proposal development.

I showed them the organizational structure, where we had relationships, the history of the account, including the current and past product installations, and our current competitors doing business there. We had a good exchange about what was working well and what we were doing as a company to support the kind of installation National Products needed with this project.

I then laid out the project parameters and the project goals and specifications, and gave them copies of the production quality internal audit so they could review the requirements.

Our Team Assessment

Everyone agreed that we needed to specifically address each of National Products' project goals (basically their business needs) with our documented results at National Products and elsewhere to support our recommendations. In short, we needed to be able to justify their investment, show them that we had their business interests in mind, and demonstrate that we were committed to getting the results they wanted.

It wasn't hard for us to come up with the technical specs and identify the spray gun systems that best fit their requirements because they had provided a lot of details in the RFI, the audit, and other documentation. Two of our newly released product designs would solve their throughput, efficiency, and quality goals. Knowing that High Beam didn't have some of the features built into our products, we spent some time on how to showcase our advantage.

From there, we broke each of the project goals down so we could tie our solution to National Products' targeted outcomes—throughput, for instance. The audit disclosed that efficiency of the existing spray guns was dropping because of their outdated design. The company had made improvements to other components of their assembly line, and the overall system was producing at a higher level, but the painting stage was not, which affected throughput. Our analysis showed that, on average, they were producing 500 units a day. Their project goal of a 5% improvement rate would mean an additional 25 per day. In similar situations we have achieved 10% and as much as 15%, so we just needed to back that up.

We did the same exercise for the defects and refinishing goal. We knew that our spray guns were putting out a more even spray that measurably reduced the number of runs or over-sprays (which can sometimes be attributed to the guns, but also to operator error). Regardless, we could quantify how the new guns resulted in fewer maintenance events. We had energy savings test data to back up our energy and sustainability compliance. And of course, our maintenance report software had been upgraded with new reporting features that would meet their needs for greater production visibility.

We all felt good, and each of us had an assignment to work on and a way to contribute. The team was excited and very confident! We agreed to reconvene in two weeks, compile the proposal, and prepare the presentation.

Customer Communication

As frequently as possible, I reached out to my contacts at National to learn everything I could to help me anticipate or spot an issue. In mid-August I sat down with Chet to share with him a straw man of what we believed would be the right approach (of course without revealing all of our thinking). I even threw out some high-level cost parameters to see if there was a reaction.

Chet was supportive and said we were headed in the right direction. He added a few things to it and said that it represented what he believed the company needed. When I asked what the process would be for presenting our proposal, he said he understood that the manufacturing team, procurement, finance, and engineering would all be represented in the meeting. They would hear both proposals and then take about a week before reconvening and making the final recommendation to executive management.

From there the recommendation would be given to the executive committee for sign-off. An expenditure of this size would often involve the CFO and CEO—I expected that. With the exception of procurement (always fixated on price) most of the people in the room would understand the technical and operational requirements and would, I believed, fairly evaluate our capabilities to meet their needs and the value we deliver. Best of all, I was feeling like I had control of the situation (as much as you can from the outside looking in). If the key to landing a big piece of business is to make sure you mitigate your risks by leveraging information and relationships every step of the way, we were in good shape!

Getting a Meeting with the CFO

Pat really encouraged me to pursue a meeting with EVP Rich Bacus and CFO John Fuller before the proposal was due. You always know, in a situation like this, that if you go above the folks who sponsor and support you, you run the risk of usurping their authority. It can backfire politically. But you also know that if you don't get to the executives, you can get blindsided later on.

I called Chet to set up a meeting. If I was going to get his help setting up a meeting with the leadership team, I needed to ask for it face-to-face, where I could respond in person to any resistance. I positioned it with Chet as a way of supporting his own efforts by sharing our commitment to National Products. I told him that in the meeting with the EVP and CEO we would outline the myriad ways we have supported the production team, solved problems, and generally delivered tremendous value. In addition, I told him, we wanted to make sure that the leadership team had a chance to meet our VP of sales, Pat Farris, out of courtesy. Chet readily agreed, to my immense relief. It took about two weeks, but we finally confirmed a 30-minute meeting with Rich and John.

My objective for that meeting was to make absolutely certain that we understood exactly why they felt they need for the Production Quality Improvement Initiative and how they viewed our company. We wanted to reiterate our advantages in areas like our installed base and our superior systems, as well as show our continued commitment.

It was a good meeting. They stated what we knew—that they were trying to improve quality to avoid some of the rising cost issues and lost revenue. They seemed very focused on having better reporting, which I believed was something our maintenance software helped them do. We left feeling good about our relationship and the opportunity for our key differentiators to meet their needs. I felt good knowing that when the production team takes their recommendation to these guys, they would sign off on it.

The Game Changed

In my view, everything was going along well. We had our proposal and presentation outlined and were waiting for the date when we could get in to present. Our meeting with Rich and John had solidified our position with them.

Then, we got a curve ball. In late September we were informed that both companies would be presenting to the executive team, which would include the CEO, CFO, head of manufacturing, head of procurement, and the chief technology officer (CTO). It was a little disconcerting because it came out of nowhere. We had understood it would be a presentation to the manufacturing operations leadership team, which would in turn make a recommendation for sign-off by the CFO and CEO. Rich and John hadn't mentioned this in our meeting with them.

I wasn't worried about our proposal or our approach, but it was a surprise. And of course there is always a risk when getting in front of the CEO and CFO, when your main relationships are elsewhere. It was added pressure for sure. Check that—it was a lot of added pressure.

Their explanation for the change was that with the size of this commitment the leaders wanted to make sure they got a clear understanding of the two companies, their approaches, and how the systems would be installed and managed going forward. No problem. We felt prepared and still in the driver's seat given our approach, pricing, relationships, and current installed base. It is hard to remove an incumbent who's been a good partner, and we were confident we had been.

Our Solution

I built the proposal and presentation around my three strategies. First, we laid out the value of what we had delivered over the past five years, including four major troubleshooting situations that shortened downtime by as much as two days, resulting in real labor savings—conservatively $250,000, we calculated. We had provided hands-on training to about 20 operators at no charge over the past two years that we figured was worth at least $50,000 that National Products hadn't had to spend from their own pocket. We knew that better training meant fewer mistakes, but we couldn't really confirm that. Still, we were up to $300,000 in hard-dollar savings.

We were able to get production data from 2011 through 2012 and discovered that our installed systems had improved their throughput by at least four pieces of additional product per assembly line per day. At four pieces per 12 assembly lines per day at 240 production days a year, that meant 11,520 pieces gained at a value of $57 per piece—or $656,640—and that was using their numbers! We were now up to $956,640 in total dollar impact.

Next we provided a total solution approach: the spray gun systems, installation services, maintenance management software, and an ongoing equipment servicing program for two years. The total came to $5,210,800, which broke down this way:

- 20 spray gun systems @ $247,540 = $4,950,800
- Installation of 20 lines @ $10,000 = $200,000
- Maintenance software @ 10,000 = $10,000
- Two-year equipment service program @ $2,500 per 20 lines = $50,000

We also estimated the change-over expense should they go with another supplier: an additional $100,000, plus the cost of retraining operators and resetting maintenance reporting protocols. Then the cost to retrofit the electrical and return systems we estimated at an additional 10 labor hours per line, or 200 hours total. We didn't have actuals, but we used an estimate of $100 per employee hour with benefits, for another $20,000.

Finally, we did the math on their goals for increased throughput, reduced downtime, fewer defects and energy savings. We knew that we could exceed their numbers, and could have gone with the higher numbers, but we stayed conservative and made sure we could defend their numbers. We felt they were ambitious and saw no need to go out on a limb.

We were aggressive on pricing, purposely positioning ourselves for a competitive bid from High Beam, but according to Joyce from finance, we had built in our desired margins. We were ready.

The Pitch

It was the morning of October 7 and the big day was here. I was pleased that we were presenting first. Every situation is different, and typically going last is best so that you can provide the big bang and answer questions that in a sense are rebuttals to your competitor. But in this case, I felt we had the upper hand with relationships and our solution, and that by pounding home the installed base we could define the decision criteria in our favor, for which High Beam would not have an answer.

I brought the "A-team": Lamar Johnson, our EVP of sales, for an executive presence from our side; Pat Farris, who is very familiar with National Products; and Lily Chang, who could speak about our products, installation, and process for integrating our equipment into their manufacturing process. I had years of experience inside their organization, so I could demonstrate a deep knowledge of their business and what they were trying to accomplish.

We had a plan and a strategy for how best to deliver our message. We had a PowerPoint presentation and kept it brief, knowing executives don't want to see 50 slides. We defined our roles. I would kick it off, make introductions, and make the presentation. Lamar would add color and listen for key messages or clues on how the National Products executives were responding to our solution. Lily would join in on the technical details, including one slide that provided an overview of our product development vision, including products in development that would support their business going forward.

I also had a handout with more detailed backup, but I didn't distribute that until I had presented the key solution components for fear they would jump ahead or get lost in the details.

National Products had five executives in the room, including Harold Roth, CEO; John Fuller, CFO; Rich Bacus, EVP of manufacturing; Mike O'Shea, CTO; and Vijay Dalal, head of procurement. After a little ice-breaking everyone was conversational and friendly. I led with my three strategies, starting with the $1 million in economic value we had delivered over the past three years by troubleshooting paint application problems and more. I had a slide with four quotes from plant managers who told us that Quality Brands had "saved their bacon," and I embellished it with a picture of sizzling hot bacon to add a little levity. The big number and the testimonies gave us a lot of credibility for their quality improvement focus, and they showed that we were committed at the ground level to help their organization be successful.

I then went through our recommended solution, including the specific spray gun systems, pumps, and all of the ancillary products that accompany them, and I covered the technical advantages we offered. Best of all, I was able to show how seamless our installation would be because of our installed base, and how we would make it an easy process. I spoke to the breadth and depth of our relationship—from the executives to the shop floor—and how much time and investment we had made in knowing their plants, working with their operators, and supporting their production goals.

I felt it went really well. Harold Roth had only a couple of questions about the impact on the production cycle and whether installation would cause any shortfall in output. Rich Bacus seemed to be very interested in the integration with current assembly line hardware and equipment. I couldn't really read his reaction, but he did seem engaged. Vijay was pretty quiet; I think he was along for the ride since the CEO and CFO were driving the process. I wasn't too worried about his reaction.

If anybody raised a worry for me, it was John Fuller, the CFO. As you would expect, he really dug into the numbers. But he seemed more concerned about the maintenance software. How robust is it, what are its reporting capabilities, and how would it affect their overall production? He and Mike O'Shea, the CTO, asked a number of questions about it. We answered their questions well, but I did leave wondering if there was something more to it.

In the end, our team all felt that our numbers, relationship, and the tone and tenor of the meeting favored us for sure. Our familiarity with their organization definitely helped establish us as the highly valued—and valuable—incumbent.

The Decision

I will never forget that day. It was one week later and I got an email from Chet saying he needed to speak to me. I thought, I hoped, that it would be good news. I called him right away, but as usual I got his voice mail. I left a message, and it was more than two hours before I heard back—a painful two hours.

The first thing he said was, "I have some bad news. The executive team has decided to go with High Beam Industries for the retrofit project." He said the main reason was that they came in with a plan to address the short-term requirements as well as a long-term strategy to upgrade all of the spray systems at all 42 plants over the next 18 months. They had also included their new Intelligent Monitor software program, which seamlessly integrates with the new enterprise resource planning (ERP) system National Products had installed early last year.

He added, "John Fuller had been searching for ways to leverage the ERP investment and to realize its overall value to the company. I can tell you High Beam made a strong case, especially the ROI they presented. Harold Roth, and especially John, bought into it completely. It absolutely was a game changer. We really didn't believe going in that the executives would think that far out of the box on this."

Chet went on to say that during the internal discussion it was clear that Rich had bought in, and that kind of sealed the deal. He said, "I am sorry, but we voiced our preferences with all the executives going into that meeting, including your history and the level of service we have received from you guys, especially you. But frankly, it came down to the overall impact the team saw with High Beam's solution."

My Reaction

I wanted to throw up. I was counting on this deal, and for three months I poured myself into it. I knew at this point that I needed to ask a few questions, the right questions to see first if I could redress the executive team's needs with a response. Perhaps I could open the door for one more conversation before the deal was signed. That would give me time to get my team together and formulate a strategy.

I needed to understand why. Not just for my sake, even though this would have been the biggest deal I have ever closed, but also because I knew that I would have to call Pat and give him the news. I know him well. He would be calm and discerning, but I also know that, as a strong salesperson, he would want me to ask the right questions to get the information he would need to get back in front of the executives. I felt I needed to find a way to resurrect this deal. I mean, this really sucked.

Chet said he would inquire to see if there was an angle we could take. He also said that he would be able to provide more details in a day or two. But he wasn't very encouraging, essentially saying, I love you guys, this was decided, and there doesn't appear to be a circumstance that would change that.

Chet did get us a meeting. Given the size of this deal and out of respect for our relationship, he said Rich and John would be pleased to meet to discuss their decision. Chet said, "Perhaps that will be a chance for you guys to reopen the discussion. But I have to tell you in all my years with the company, I have never seen the executive team go back on a final decision. But hey, I will do whatever I can to help you prepare for that meeting."

The Aftermath

Lamar and I went in to meet with John Fuller and Rich Bacus. We were able to get a high-level understanding of what High

Beam sold them. We were a bit shocked that we hadn't known about the new Intelligent Monitor software. Obviously, that caught us and the market off guard. Good job by them. Still, we felt that our software was strong enough to accomplish what they needed in the short term, and we were working on a similar product. But mostly we went back through the risks and costs of changing suppliers and systems, and how such a change might not deliver the results promised.

It was a good exchange. Both were open, honest, and willing to debate it. But in the end, their minds were made up. When that happens, it's almost impossible to turn things around. One thing really stood out to me: They kept reiterating the profit improvement, the impact on margins, and the value of the new software for managing cash, leveraging the ERP, and giving senior management greater visibility. I knew we had hit them with a strong financial story, but whatever High Beam did really won them over. I needed to learn more about the profit impact and what they meant when they said High Beam had showed them how to achieve it.

We of course offered our services during the transition. We assured them that we would like to remain a resource and would definitely like an opportunity to bring new ideas and products when appropriate.

It is never easy losing a deal. It is harder to lose a deal to a direct competitor. But it is hardest of all to lose a deal to a competitor who was able to completely beat you at your own game. That's what High Beam did. During our debrief meeting with Rich and John we learned that High Beam had just released a new version of their maintenance monitoring software that included a new technology for wireless connectivity down to the actual spray gun system, integrated with ERP for real-time enterprise-wide reporting.

I knew from my experience with National Products that the company was very focused on centralized data. Our software supported that, and I never felt that we didn't provide what they needed. But I also knew they had invested in a new ERP system that gave them an integrated real-time view of their core business processes such as production, order processing, and inventory management. I was surprised that National Products saw our spray gun systems as being undifferentiated from High Beam's. I know ours are better, but it didn't seem to matter.

The worst part was losing a deal that our executive management was invested in and that was set to define my career with Quality Brands. Oh well, that didn't work out. But, out of a loss always springs new insight.

....

The following discussion between Quality Brands' CEO Jim Thomas and Lamar Johnson after the meeting with National Products captures the new level of understanding by Quality Brands about how they needed to compete and sell going forward.

Jim: How did your meeting go?

Lamar: The meeting went well, but we didn't get the result we were looking for. They wouldn't move on their decision. We pointed out that we felt we weren't given a full opportunity to propose a broader long-term solution.

Jim: What was their response?

Lamar: Well, they said that it wasn't their initial intention but that High Beam made such a compelling case and backed it up with a strategy, data, and financials that completely changed their calculus. Though I offered a passionate defense of our capabilities to accomplish the same outcome, even I had to admit it sounded like I was whining.

Jim: What is your takeaway from this experience now that you've done an autopsy of the situation?

This deal would never have happened had I not been able to get to the CFO John Fuller when I did. I am not sure we were even on their radar early on, and given the fact that I had virtually no relationships with the manufacturing side of the house, it was a long shot. But once I found a way to get to John, and then learn what I believe his hot buttons were, I had a pretty clear path to follow.

I have done some million-dollar deals in the past, but this one was the largest with the biggest odds against us. I think that's what makes this so rewarding personally for me. I really had to get creative and be bold to win this deal with the help of a great team.

My Relationships

I got this account 60 days before we learned about National Products' quality improvement project, and frankly, I think we had been left for dead. We had some success at National Products a number of years ago, but because of a lack of attention and presence in the account, we lost most of the business we had to Quality Brands, which has been in there working hard to grow the business.

They had a lot of longstanding relationships that I didn't have when I arrived. All I had was a purchasing agent in procurement and a plant manager in Texas where we still had a system operating, although they were planning to replace it. I did try to get to Rich Bacus, the executive vice president of manufacturing, but he pushed me down to Lester Powers, who is vice president of manufacturing. After repeated and unsuccessful attempts to reach Lester, I called Chet Gretzky, the director of manufacturing operations. I had been told that Chet was the go-to guy on all things spray gun–related.

Chet is a nice guy. He was very cordial but not very open to considering High Beam. Nonetheless, we did schedule some time to meet. The meeting went well, but he basically said that National Products had been extremely pleased with Quality Brands and that there was little chance that the company would go in a new direction at this point. He left the door open a little bit by saying that as we introduce new products or technology, he would be open to hearing about it and sharing it with others in manufacturing.

So, I was left to my own devices to try and get to someone who would champion our cause. My initial thought was to keep trying to get to the EVP of manufacturing or even the CEO or CFO. But first I needed better intelligence about what was going on at National Products. I decided to go back to the one National plant where we still have a system in place to see if that plant's manager could help me navigate the company.

The National Products Company Initiative

It was a real stroke of luck that I ever found out about the Production Quality Improvement Initiative. In mid-June my contact in procurement emailed me to ask if High Beam would be bidding on the new project because an RFI was going out soon. I didn't know anything about it, so I called him to see what he could tell me. He didn't know much and frankly seemed a little close to the vest about it.

I think he may have found out after contacting me that it wasn't certain that there would be an RFP and he didn't want to get in trouble by communicating to suppliers prematurely. It was good luck that we heard about it when we did. Chances were, based on Quality Brands' penetration in the account and their relationships, this deal could easily have happened without our even knowing about it. That is scary to think about now.

Rob Hernandez was the plant manager in Austin, Texas, where we still had a system operating, he had been a fan of ours over the years, but unfortunately we hadn't done a good job of maintaining the relationship over the past few years. I asked him to give me the information on National Products' production quality project. He knew that leadership had conducted an audit to identify ways to improve quality, and he had heard that 20 of their 42 plants were being considered for a spray gun system upgrade. That would be a huge project—$3 to $4 million, I thought at the time. I asked if he had a copy of the audit, and he said no but would look into getting me one.

He said he understood there were a number of paint application problems and that more product was being sent to repaint and touch up. I knew that would be painful from a couple of standpoints. First, it slows down production. Second, it slows down revenue and ties up cash in inventory that can't be shipped quickly. Plus, it adds to operating costs.

One thing stood out in our conversation with Rob: There seemed to be a heavy emphasis on maintenance and repair, and on monitoring and reporting. He had been included in an IT project recently that analyzed their plant production reporting process. With the ERP investment they made last year, leadership was searching for ways to leverage the system.

A bell went off when I heard that. I had just closed a deal with a company that integrated our new Intelligent Monitor software with their ERP system. I noted that for further research. At least I was getting some information. Up to this point I had been flying blind.

My Internal Discussions

I called Carl Kim, my vice president of North American sales, to give him a heads-up about the National Products opportunity. On one hand, I was excited to tell him about it. On the other hand, I wondered if drawing attention to an account with a large opportunity where we had few relationships would reflect poorly on us, especially considering the fact we didn't know about it until very late in the game. I mean, you create all this energy around the potential of a big deal while quietly knowing the probability is low. Then it ends up feeling like a major fire drill for nothing. But, I thought, there's no need in dwelling on that. It was now about competing and seeing if we could strike gold.

Carl was familiar with this account and had even made a few sales calls on them a year ago or so with the last account manager that handled National Products. He said he could sense at the time that Quality Brands had been very active in the account and had built strong relationships on the manufacturing and production side of the house. Nonetheless, he wanted to give it our full attention and see if we could get our hat in the ring.

I explained to him that I didn't have a lot of information yet but that it was a quality improvement initiative aimed at upgrading their aging spray gun systems. I also told him there might be a unique angle that would favor High Beam—National Products' effort to integrate their maintenance and production reporting with their new ERP System.

Carl suggested a conference call with Javier Munoz, vice president of product development, as well as our CTO Ben Karan, to get their input, and to get this opportunity on their radar to ensure we'd have the resources we needed. Following that, we would regroup and start outlining a strategy to win this deal. We scheduled a one-on-one call to update my progress.

My One-on-One with Carl Kim

Carl has done deals like this many times in his career and was quick to establish some next steps to help guide me through the process. He said we needed to compensate for our lack of relationships at National Products by doing a particularly thorough job in the discovery phase of analyzing the account.

Since I was so new to the account, he knew that doing a good job of learning about the executives and the company's business, financials, and operations would build credibility with leadership. I prided myself in analyzing a customer's business; that was one of my strengths.

Carl had spent time in the strategic accounts group before being promoted to vice president, so he had a process he always went through. His list of to-do's for me included:

1. Analyze their business—not just their recent earnings, but really dig into what is happening with this company, what the trends are, who their competitors are, changes in leadership, strategy, acquisitions, you name it. Ultimately, it was about learning how we could align with executives and show how we could deliver hard-dollar profit improvement.

2. Scope and budget—Learn more about the scope and budget for this project so we could start planning our approach. Too often projects get derailed because the price tag isn't known or, as it evolved, scope creep killed the initiative.

3. Decision making—Find out what the decision-making process will be. We needed to know who we needed to get to and/or influence if we were to have any chance of getting in on this project and winning it; we needed to know when a decision would be made and when they wanted to install the systems.

4. Competition—Find out which competitors are pursuing this business, and do our due diligence on them.

5. Resources—Pull together the internal resources we would need to spec out the project and ensure that we could deliver.

And that was just for starters!

My Next Steps

I had my work cut out for me, but it was exciting. I didn't have anything to lose. It was like being on the team that wasn't expected to be in the playoffs, playing free and easy, making all the plays, and secretly hoping to celebrate a world championship that no one really believed was possible.

I took Carl's advice, and I will be immodest—I did a good job of analyzing National Products' business from an operational, business, and financial perspective. I knew it had paid off when National Products' CEO said later, after my presentation, that he hadn't seen a salesperson take the time to understand their business at the level I did. He said my presentation was really effective because I related everything I was recommending back to their financial goals. That was quite a compliment.

I pride myself on doing that well. Of course, I come by it honestly. My father, CFO of a Fortune 500 company for 25 years, told me when I got my first sales job that he had one piece of advice for me. He said, *"If you want to be successful at your job, make sure you learn how to break down a customer's financials. I don't mean just looking at the income statement to see how much money they made or didn't make. To be effective with executives you need to speak their language. As CFO, what I know from my experience with salespeople over the years is that they always come in focused on what they sell and not on how what they sell impacts our profitability or our cash flow or our ability to grow the business. There is not a decision we make that isn't driven by economics. If you can understand a customer's business and interpret their strategies relative to their revenue goals, cost management objectives, and capital plans, then you will set yourself apart from 90% of all the salespeople out there."*

I took his advice to heart, and I have had some great mentors who taught me how to look at a customer's business. One of my first sales managers spent time in the finance department before getting into sales. He coached me on breaking down the business into simple-to-understand elements.

My Discovery Process

I have a set of steps I follow during the discovery phase of my sales process. I start with the customer's 10-K report, the annual report mandated by the Securities and Exchange Commission. In it, a company describes their business in their own words, which gives you the cadence and context of how they talk about their business internally. And the information it provides is rich.

Companies describe their strategies, market segments, and competition. They break down their reporting segments, which can help you identify who the highest P&L leaders are by division. They may disclose who their largest customers are and what percentage of their overall business each major customer represents. If those customers are your customers, you might make connections with their most valued revenue sources. The 10K form will have industry trends, key strategies, and of course their risk factors. Knowing their risk factors is valuable because they provide clues to vulnerabilities. If you match those with their market, operational, or industry challenges, you can often focus your solution on something that directly impacts profitability.

My Financial Analysis

I looked at National Products' 10-K and their consolidated income statement. I wanted to know if they were growing as a company. In my analysis of their business and their direct competitors I wanted to know if they were growing faster than the market. Were they growing faster than competition? Were they gaining market share? Were they growing as fast as they predicted or at the levels they forecast to Wall Street and to shareholders? I tried to think like an analyst who was deciding whether to invest in this company. That helped me filter the information and prepare questions that I used to get a better understanding of their business issues.

As it turned out, National Products' revenues were basically flat and their gross margins were significantly down. Right out of the gate I knew there was pain. The cause could be the economy, or maybe they were getting beaten by competitors, or losing customers, or not bringing new products to market fast enough. Whatever the cause, I knew I needed to figure it out so I could figure out how we might impact it.

I then looked at costs. Are they operating their business profitably? Because they are a manufacturer, I wanted to know what was happening with the cost of goods sold (COGS), an important metric because it affects gross profits. If raw materials costs are going up, or if the company's manufacturing process isn't efficient, that's a hit to gross profit. Knowing that National Products had a Production Quality Improvement Initiative, I surmised that inefficiencies in the process were a cause.

Their gross profit margin could also suffer if they were not competing well in the market and thus were unable to pass cost increases on to their customers and were thereby not protecting their pricing. When I saw that National Products' earnings reports and analyst calls had a heavy emphasis on gross profit margins, I started looking at what they were doing to control costs, to see whether I could affect them.

Seeing that their revenues were flat last year and their gross margins were down significantly, I realized that the executive team was under tremendous pressure to make short-term changes to offset the loss in margin. They needed to show analysts that they had a strategy for correcting course. Sometimes companies do, and sometimes they don't. In most cases, customers are open to ideas about how to fix the problem. At National Products I knew that anything I could do to show an impact on revenue growth and lowering the cost of goods sold would get their attention, especially if I could quantify it.

I then looked at operating costs. In their case this included labor, sales and marketing, human resources, legal, insurance, rent—all the things that help them operate the business. They talked about their operating expense ratio a lot in their financial reports, so I knew I needed to familiarize myself with that number and how it was calculated to ensure that I could include it in my approach to their solution. For most companies, operating expense ratio is operating costs as a percentage of revenue, with operating costs usually consisting of SG&A (selling, general, and administrative expenses). It's an efficiency number. Here again, National Products' operating expense ratio was ticking up, and I knew that would be another direct hit on operating income. There are a number of ways our solutions can help lower these costs, so it was up to me to find the right areas and include them in my proposal. All in all, I felt I had some good leverage to show how we could financially impact their business and, as my dad had advised, their profitability.

One final piece that a lot of salespeople miss is the customer's balance sheet. It tells me how much money they have invested in the business in the form of fixed assets (plants, offices, warehouses, etc.) or working capital (including inventory and accounts receivable). It tells me if they getting a return on capital for their shareholders. After all, a lot of capital comes from shareholders who want to know the company is managing assets well. If they have too much capital tied up in other areas, such as accounts receivable or inventory, it might be difficult for them to justify using their cash to invest in our spray gun systems.

Using LinkedIn

Most salespeople use LinkedIn, a great research tool. I looked at all of the LinkedIn profiles for the National Products executives and was delighted to find I had a key connection. Turns out that a close friend of mine, Andy Cooper, senior vice president of marketing at one of my key customers, knows National Products' CFO John Fuller well. I learned from a recommendation Andy posted on John Fuller's profile that they go back years, to the time they served together in the Marines. I hoped this was the break I needed to give me a path to a high-level contact that I had lacked. I felt that my friend could serve as a reference as I approached the National Products CFO.

I called Andy, who confirmed that he did indeed know John Fuller well; in fact, they had spent six months together on a ship. He had some funny things to say about their experience, which I thought I could use later. When he asked how he could help me, I said I was hoping he could get me an introduction, perhaps send an email to let John know that I would like to meet with him. I was eager to get High Beam into the conversation before they excluded us from their short list.

Andy asked me to send him a message with the points I wanted to communicate and promised to forward the message along with his recommendation that John take my call. Perfect. I would get National Products' attention at a high enough level to give us a fighting chance.

My Breakthrough

It worked! Here's what I did in my email for John Fuller. I didn't have enough details about the Production Quality Improvement Initiative to reference, nor any production-level contacts for insider information. So I took the approach that we wanted to be considered for the project based on the significant profit improvement we had delivered for another large global manufacturer, and I mentioned two recent successes where we had installed new spray gun systems with significant financial return.

I referenced National Products' recent quarterly earnings as well as John's comments during the Q&A part of last quarter's earnings conference call, when he was asked how they were going to grow revenue, improve gross margins, and generate stronger cash flow. I noted that I was aware of their production quality improvement effort and their plans to invest. I said I would like to share how we could improve their gross margins, reduce operating expenses through an improved maintenance process, and speed up production quality in order to significantly reduce product defects.

It got his attention. He responded to my email and asked that I contact his assistant to schedule a brief meeting. I did so right away; time was not my friend.

Getting Ready for My Meeting with the CFO

I knew I needed more information about the project so that I could go in prepared to ask good questions. I always go into a meeting like this with a plan. First, I need to connect with the executive, so the more I know about him or her, the company, and what is happening in their business, the better. But I also needed to know more about this project. So thinking there must be something documented on this I asked John Fuller's assistant if I could get a copy of their project goals, budget, timing, and so on. She said she would check with John and get back to me. I heard back the same day; she said John was fine with it, but that first we would have to sign a nondisclosure agreement since there was some proprietary information in the report. I gladly complied.

In a couple of days I received the audit and began studying it. It wasn't my intent to go in with a formal proposal because I still didn't have sufficient information. But I did feel I could go in with a proven example of how we had delivered profit improvement in organizations *like* National Products. I could give them the vision for how we would do it, and earn credibility with them. My number one objective was to get invited to the party. With a multi-million-dollar deal on the table, I wanted to make sure we were one of the companies on the short list, regardless of who else might be on it. I mean, you can't compete and win if you aren't in the game.

Then I went to YouTube—which I always do as part of my company research and analysis—and hit the jackpot.

Using YouTube

When I tell other salespeople that YouTube is a great resource for selling, I get some blank stares. But that's where you find presentations or speeches from key people that give pure insight into their business. For example, I saw one about how GE Healthcare was using unique techniques and product designs from kids to make MRIs for children more friendly and fun. It was delivered passionately by one of the senior product engineers at an industry conference. It was very informative and emotional, as it dealt with families whose children have life-threatening health problems, as well as children's fear of medical tests. In another case I saw a supply chain and logistics presentation about a privately held company. Both times I learned important facts that I couldn't find anywhere else.

So, searching YouTube for National Products and specifically John Fuller, I found a 30-minute video of him speaking at a Building Industry Trade Association conference about their innovative manufacturing processes as part of a trend toward "self-monitoring production." He talked about how, as product designs and data and technology converge, the level of centralized analytics and decision support is driving tremendous efficiencies and speed throughout the supply chain, from order to manufacturing through to delivery to customers. It was great stuff, and it revealed that John had a real bent toward technology.

This hit me like a lightning bolt. High Beam wasn't known for our innovation and especially our technology—in fact it had been a weakness for us. But I also knew that we had invested heavily in a new generation of monitoring technology. We had just released a new technology integrated with our spray gun systems that included a corporate dashboard that generated real-time data on production performance. It even had cellular technology to alert the production crew, in real time, of any anomalies. Really leading edge. While our products are good, reliable, and effective, that alone doesn't give us a big competitive advantage. But combining that with our new capability, I felt we could make a really strong business case. This was cool.

Our Ticket to the Game

Carl couldn't join me in my meeting with John Fuller, and I was a little nervous about doing it myself. When I arrived, I noticed a second person in the CFO's conference room. Turns out it was Rich Bacus, EVP of manufacturing. That could be good or bad depending on whether or not he was already in the Quality Products camp. I just didn't know, but it could be a twofer, hitting two top executives at the same time with the same message.

I can say now that my meeting with John and Rich could not have gone better. It started out with small talk; I mentioned my friend Andy's comment that he and John had had to bunk together for six weeks at sea and he was still getting over it. That broke the ice. I went on to describe my understanding of their business, their financial results, and their strategies. I told them that I understood that they wanted to grow revenue by 10%, improve margins by 2%, and speed up cash flow by $50 million, and to that end they planned to invest in their production facilities.

John confirmed those figures, as well as their quality improvement goals. Both men were open and frank. Rich mentioned the quality issues, the need for speed, and the problems with the paint application process requiring more and more repaints and touch-ups. John added his concern about the cash tied up in inventory. All in all, they laid out the reason for the project and its scope. I followed up with one of Carl's key questions: Did they budget this project for this year? John said yes, they had planned their capital budgets for the next two years and everything was in their budget.

He went on to say that one of their big needs was to improve their data. He mentioned the new ERP system and that he was particularly interested in any ideas I had for integrating production data with ERP systems. That was my opening. I mentioned his YouTube video, and he seemed impressed that I had found it and pleased I had watched it. I told him about our research and our new software release, and about how I had recently integrated the software with ERP for another client. I added that although we hadn't done a lot of business in the past few years with National Products we were eager to prove our value and the impact we could deliver.

I took the opportunity to refer to a project for which we had documented over $10 million in profit improvement that was focused on paint application quality and centralized monitoring reports. He was interested in knowing how we did that. Long story short, we had a great exchange, and near the end I flat-out told them that we wanted to have an opportunity to propose on the production quality improvement project. As I did that, I pulled out our brand new white paper, "Production Quality Monitoring Technologies— The Next Generation." Fortunately I had two copies with me. Our marketing group does a good job in supporting us, but that white paper was a home run! Their eyes got pretty big when they saw it. Rich said he would have his assistant send along the RFI information and to call him about any technical questions.

I had one more move to make. Carl had suggested pushing for a C-level review of our proposal and ideally a decision. We didn't want to submit a proposal only to the production organization, which might well ignore our solution. So I got bold and said that a staged or piecemeal approach toward improving production would typically deliver a lot less profitability than a comprehensive approach. And by comprehensive I meant a fully aligned and integrated paint application and production system with the latest equipment, and further combined with a fully integrated ERP and corporate production dashboard. I added that we could drive tremendous efficiencies immediately—as their financial goals demanded—with the power of our Intelligent Monitor software with its wireless, real-time data exchange from the corporate level to the assembly line and individual operator level.

I could tell that I had hit a nerve. John paused, thought for a minute, and said *"That is a very interesting idea."* He added those golden words, *"I would like to know how you would achieve that, what the costs would be, and what the payback is. When you submit*

your proposal, I would like to know what that option would be."
Score! That's exactly what I wanted to do: avoid an RFP that would level the playing field. Now I had a way to overcome the lack of relationships and pitch a game-changing play that could actually give us a legitimate chance at winning this project.

I thanked them both, asked if I could circle back in a few weeks with any follow-up questions, and promised that High Beam was looking forward to providing our recommendations at the executive presentation. I couldn't wait to talk to Carl.

National Products' Project Description and RFI— Request for Information

The next day I received an email with the RFI from Rich's assistant, Ann Kane, and discovered that the project parameters were actually broader than I expected. The RFI included the full scope of the Production Quality Improvement Initiative:

Project Goals
1. Increase product throughput by 5%
2. Reduce defects and/or re-finishing rates by 5%
3. Reduce production downtime due to maintenance and repairs by 10%
4. Improve energy efficiency to meet corporate sustainability goals
5. Improve maintenance monitoring and reporting

Project Specifications
- 20 Plants with 1 assembly line each = 20 lines
- 1 spray gun system (spray booths, pumps, hoses, canisters, cleaning sinks, gun racks and other accessories) per line
- Installation services (including engineering designs, change-over services)

- Maintenance management software for facility-specific equipment performance monitoring
- Ongoing equipment servicing program for parts and repair services
- All systems to be installed and operational by March 31 to correspond with the beginning of the second quarter production cycle
- The decision will be made no later than October 31

Now the heavy lifting began. I needed to gather more detailed information before our internal planning meeting. My team would need to know some of the production numbers that would make it possible to propose on this deal. Plus, I need data to build a financial case. When I got the RFI, I shot it off to Carl and Javier Munoz in Product Development. Then I made a list of information I needed from Rich Bacus:

- The number of repaints and touch-ups per line per plant
- The length of time products sit on the floor before they are refinished and ready to ship
- Lost revenue as a result of missed shipments—the big-box retailers' supply chain organization will buy from a secondary supplier if the lead supplier's shipments are delayed by 48 hours. How much does that happen?
- Over-application of paint. Estimate of the amount of excess paint per unit. Average paint cost per unit.
- Lost revenue. Do they experience product shortages due to the production cycle being interrupted?
- The number and frequency of assembly line shutdowns due to maintenance and/or equipment repair.
- The number of hours engineering spends on repairing equipment, especially during prime production time. With a maintenance and monitoring system, faults can be anticipated and the maintenance and repairs can be made

offline, in off hours, to avoid the lost labor when employees have to be idle for hours.

- Amount of inventory tied up due to an interrupted production cycle and with backups on product repainting or touch-up.

From Rich and with the help of a few other people on his staff that crunch the numbers, I was able to get the key metrics we needed to make our business case. Equipped with good information, I was feeling confident.

My Initial Strategy

My number one strategy was to change the rules of the game by making the decision about profitability. Every executive looks at a decision like this and asks, what is my return on investment, when will I see it, and how confident am I that this will work? I needed to position my solution as a financial decision, not a technical decision. Of course, I had to cover my technical bases, but knowing that we were absolutely on par with our major competitors, this deal would be about helping the customer make a good financial decision. It just happened to be around spray guns, but frankly, it could have been about delivery trucks. No matter what you sell, in the end the customer is buying the impact of what they buy, not the features of what you sell. That's the mindset I needed to maintain.

So, once I saw their financials I knew that if I could show impact on margins, costs, and cash flow I would be able to position our company. John and Rich confirmed that for me during our meeting. The audit did refer to the need for better monitoring reporting. As far as we knew, Quality Brands did not have an integrated, centralized, cloud-based monitoring software with wireless capability. So my game changer was Intelligent Monitor. With that I could build a solution and a profit improvement strategy that would upgrade all of National Products' spray gun systems across their manufacturing facilities, and install and integrate our Intelligent Monitor production quality software with ERP. They could realize huge profit improvement results quickly.

I was so glad that High Beam had invested in that software. It was a stroke of genius that I felt would be the difference-maker in this deal, because if I could show how the monitoring system could drive profitability—that is, profitability gains in areas they hadn't mentioned in their audit—then we could capture their imagination. If we could show product superiority, or at the very least, product parity, our approach and software just might be the brass ring here. My job was to get more information on the operational factors driving their financial outcomes.

The other thing I wanted to have in my back pocket was National Products' Water Filtration Division. I read that they were working on a new WOW (War on Waste) initiative and that sustainability, energy, and eco-audits needed to be integrated. We had a module that could tie all divisions together—filtration and quality water system with their fixtures. I didn't want to distract from the main initiative, but being able to share a vision for how we could reach farther into their organization would tee me up for future business, if not help me close this deal.

The Proposal Review Process

I got an email from Ann Kane inviting us to present High Beam's production quality improvement project solution to the executive team on the afternoon of October 7. Copied on the distribution list, so I assumed also invited to the meeting, were John Fuller, CFO; Rich Bacus, EVP of manufacturing; Harold Roth, CEO; Mike O'Shea, CTO; and Lester Powers, director of manufacturing operations. I felt invigorated by that. We had taken this deal from an inside job with influencers driving the bus to an open forum with the final decision makers. This is the way we wanted it, and I was pleased that we got it. Our probability of winning this deal just went up by 50%, perhaps more.

The Competition

In the situation we were in, I actually didn't think that much about our competitor. Knowing it was Quality Brands, I felt that we knew a lot about their products, their value proposition, and what they were doing at National Products. We knew that they had 60% or 70% of the business. We knew that they had a lot of relationships, although I didn't think they were spending a lot of time in the executive suite. They seemed to be very focused on the production team and serving their needs. Besides, since I was attempting to completely change the game, we would be comparing apples to oranges. Still, we had a hunch that they would focus on their history, relationships, and the fact that they were the incumbent and would probably make the case for not changing suppliers and systems. They had better production data than I had, so I was going to have to make some leaps of faith on that, but I still hoped I could get more data.

The Decision-Making Process

Once I knew that we would present our solution to the executive team after Quality Brands, I was encouraged. I felt we could dictate the decision process by introducing a big profit improvement number that would change the calculation for making the investment. By connecting with John and Rich on the technology and introducing a new way of viewing their business, I felt that there would be less focus on the technical side of the spray gun systems and more on enterprise-wide productivity and executive visibility into the ERP and production quality reporting. I was banking on a financial decision and not a technical or relationship decision.

The Team Planning Meeting

I was excited about our meeting. Going in I felt I had a strong strategy for winning this business. But now I was with the experts, and if what I was thinking was not possible, I was screwed. When I described my vision, it was the boldest I have ever been. But what the heck, I went in as the underdog and this was probably my only chance of winning. The team reacted positively. They were all excited about my proposed approach. Fortunately, I have a great team that is open and collaborative. If there was a way our team could figure it out, they would.

They had all seen and studied the RFI and the audit. In the meeting besides our Sales VP Carl Kim and our Product Development VP Javier Munoz, I had Sunita Patel, who is our technology liaison and who probably knows more about production monitoring technology then anyone in the entire industry, and Ben Cohen, who works in our sales operations area and crunches our numbers for proposals, sales and customer performance reports, and more.

I reviewed the status of the opportunity, where we were, and how we got there. I reviewed in detail the meeting I had with the executives and laid out my premise—the game-changing approach. Javier had really done his homework. He had worked with our installation staff and Ben Cohen to lay out the entire vision for an enterprise-wide installation over an 18-month period. Why 18 months? First, because we couldn't do it faster, and second, we thought the customer wouldn't buy the enterprise-wide installation. It was crazy-aggressive but given that our company needed revenue and everyone was feeling the heat, it was energizing and flat-out exhilarating.

We went over National Products' business goals. One by one, we knocked them out.

1. Increase product throughput by 5%. *We had documentation validating that the combination of our software and spray gun monitoring would exceed this.*
2. Reduce defects and/or refinishing rates by 5%. *We believed we could exceed this by 10%.*
3. Reduce production downtime due to maintenance and repairs by 10%. *This would be a big win for us because of our monitoring software. We could document the labor and time associated with each event.*
4. Improve energy efficiency to meet corporate sustainability goals. *We didn't have a lot of internal data on this, but we were able to estimate power savings based on some public data we found.*
5. Improve maintenance monitoring and reporting. *The game changer—need I say more?*

I then reviewed the information that Rich and his staff provided me on production, labor, and more, which helped us quantify some of the areas that would support the profitability impact of our solution.

Our Solution

If I could change the conversation from building on Quality Brands' strong position and installed base to a game-changing approach that would deliver significant profitability, I felt I would have an edge. I knew from the audit what the basic metrics were, that Quality Brands would be emphasizing their performance, throughput, and quality. But knowing that we were at least six months to a year ahead of them in the new corporate production quality monitoring software system, I felt I could use some other key data and double up on the profit impact by introducing new and different metrics.

For example, I knew that over-application of paint was a big problem. I was able to find out that there was a significant amount of over-painting occurring across the system, even with some of the more current spray guns they were using. If you include the cost of paint, which is expensive, the labor and downtime during recalibration, and the slowdown in throughput, there was as much as $600,000 per plant in avoidable costs. In our proposal, we stayed conservative at $500,000 per plant. This included labor and other costs.

Next, I knew that touch-up or refinishing was a problem. How often was that needed? How long does each product sit on the floor (I was thinking cash tied up, and at the cost of capital that could be worth x). I needed some frame of reference on that.

We were also conservative in calculating the cost of converting all of National Products' assembly line spray gun systems over the next 18 months. We provided a total solution approach that included the spray gun systems, installation services, Intelligent Monitor software, integration maintenance management software, and an ongoing equipment servicing program for two years. The total came to $12,215,100, which broke down this way:

- 42 spray gun systems @ $274,600 = $11,533,200
- Installation of 42 lines @ $11,750 = $493,500
- Intelligent Monitor software and ERP integration services @ 75,000 = $75,000
- Three-year equipment service program @ $2,700 per 42 lines = $113,400
- Terms
    —$8 million in year one, 60% of the systems installed
    —Full integration of the Intelligent Monitor software with ERP in the first 60 days
    —$5 million in year two, 40% of remaining systems installed
    —$500,000 in year three for ongoing maintenance and support

I knew that the ERP system gave National Products an integrated real-time view of its core business processes such as production, order processing, and inventory management, tied together by ERP applications software and a common database maintained by a database management system. These systems tracked business resources (such as cash, production capacity, and raw materials) and the status of the commitments they make (such as customer orders, purchase orders, and employee payroll). I knew that no matter which department (manufacturing, purchasing, sales, accounting, and so on) enters data into the system, ERP facilitates information flow between all business functions inside the organization and manages connections to outside stakeholders. That is what Intelligent Monitor will integrate with and support. That was our silver bullet.

The Pitch

It was the afternoon of October 7. We checked in with security at the National Products corporate offices. It was a sunny day, a good omen. I was pleased we were presenting second, because it gave us the opportunity to change the game without a direct rebuttal.

With me I had Carl Kim, Ralph Morris (EVP of sales), and Javier Munoz. I had our proposal, copies of selected pages from our presentation, and an iPad for each executive. I also brought a wireless modem so that the executives could individually connect to our server to review prototype reports from our Intelligent Monitor software using data based on the production quality management metrics we had received from Rob Hernandez, the plant manager in Austin, Texas. I intended to save that for last, after we hit them with the profit impact of our solution, the product and technical specifications of our recommendations for the entire manufacturing system, and the software. That would be the bow on our package. Then we would return to the financial pages and show how we arrived at the $27 million profit improvement.

We all got introduced and everyone settled in. This was my first time meeting Lester Powers, who was part of the production management team that Quality Brands was so close to. I couldn't read him well, as he was pretty reserved. But everyone else seemed open, conversational, and interested to hear our presentation. At least, that's the way I read it.

Right out of the gate I hit them with the most important number of the day, $27 million in profit improvement as a result of converting their enterprise-wide spray gun system. The plan would be to deliver $27 million in additional operating income in year one and add another $10 million over the following two years through what we proposed under the title *Data Fusion— Integrated Production Quality Monitoring System.* It would require 18 months to install all of the system upgrades and updates, putting them on the same footing with some of the world's most advanced manufacturing companies who are driving production efficiencies, supply chain optimization, and product quality improvement through their ERP and technology organizations.

I broke down the impact of more efficient production, speed, and quality. I showed how inventory building up across all plants was increasing and that when product is pulled off for repainting or touch-up, it ties up capital and increases costs. I showed them how their business with the big-box home improvement companies was at risk when product delivery became an issue. We had data showing that when product isn't available, those big buyers take the next supplier on the list to ensure that they have inventory stocked at the stores and on the floor.

I also made a big point about the application over-spray; the application of paint at higher densities dramatically drives up paint costs, which in turn has a significant impact on the cost of goods sold and, of course, gross margin. Plainly said, over-spray was making them uncompetitive.

The numbers broke down this way: To recapture or avoid lost revenue at $51 million annually, I used their 13.3% operating margin, so that was worth over $6.8 million. We estimated the profitability gained by eliminating the costs of excess paint, lost direct labor hours, and more to be over $500,000 annually per plant, or $21 million, which brought the total to $27 million. We added $250,000 per plant for labor savings due to less downtime during repairs and maintenance (thanks to Intelligent Monitor), which added over $9.7 million. Finally, we estimated a decrease of $20 million in inventory, which improved cash flow; with the cost of capital at 10%, that was another $2 million. Finally, we showed that the Intelligent Monitor software would reduce operating expenses by reducing time spent at the plant and regional and corporate level crunching; and manual reporting on production quality and maintenance would be avoided altogether. The grand total was around $39 million in profitability. After we subtracted the $12 million investment to deploy our enterprise-wide system and software, they would net $27 million in profit improvement. Best of all, we showed that it was based on *their* numbers, *their* data.

Then I had our CTO, Ben Karan, cover the conversion strategy, technical specs, and performance of our spray gun systems. He showed recent research on our quality, reliability, ease of use, and operator training. He compared High Beam's maintenance and repair standards, which had improved in each of the last three years, with those of other industry leaders like Quality Brands. Basically, Ben answered the question, "Why High Beam?" That was powerful and effective. I could see that Rich was totally engaged. Lester was too. That was a pleasant surprise, because until then I had viewed him as a possible mole for the competitor.

Now it was time for the run on the palace. The big enchilada, the game-changing Hail Mary. I handed out the iPads and said that we could demonstrate the benefits of our total solution approach by viewing our Intelligent Monitor software, which brings all of the conversion and enterprise-wide production data to a single desktop. And, using my cell phone, we demonstrated the wireless feature that notifies the system that the paint quantities have been exceeded, which in turn triggers the paint application calibration faults, pausing the system. It will also notify the system that there has been an unscheduled shutdown—all of which, I added, is fully integrated with your ERP system. We purposely included an inventory management report and other logistics data to show how the system supports the entire supply chain management process.

Was it a hit? They were blown away. It wasn't a home run—it was a grand slam in the bottom of the ninth inning of the seventh game of the World Series.

Now it was time for questions and answers. I wasn't sure what to expect, but we felt ready. Rich asked a few questions about the process and timing of shutting down plants to convert. Lester added a few follow-ups around technical and logistical aspects. John wanted to know about timing of the installations and the investment. Clearly, he was working out how he could fund this based on all of their other priorities. Harold Roth, the CEO, was fairly quiet. He seemed to defer to John and Rich, which was fine with me. I felt a connection, and the level of enthusiasm for the total systems approach seemed to resonate.

Since I had my sales manager and EVP of sales in the room, I knew I would be remiss if I didn't ask for the business. So, I finished up by saying, *"I know that we came in today and presented a very aggressive solution. I also know that, based on your financial goals, you guys are not just thinking about incremental changes here and there. We are 100% certain that we can deliver $27 million in year one of this agreement. We are 100% certain that we can deliver our systems on time, and we are 100% certain that we can deliver industry-leading executive decision support technology that accelerates your ongoing quality and efficiency goals. Most of all, we are vying to become an earnings contributor to your organization. We would like your business on this project, and the chance to build a profitable relationship for years to come. I hope you will choose us for this very important project."*

With that we wrapped up. I got immediate positive feedback: *"Great presentation. You gave us a lot to think about. Good job."* And finally: *"We will get back to you with our decision within the next seven to ten days."* Whew!

The Decision

It was October 14 and I was getting nervous. I hadn't heard anything, and I wondered if there were any hiccups. One thing I have learned is that time kills deals. It was like being an attorney waiting for the jury to return with a verdict. Was more or less time a good sign? I tried not to agonize over that.

Then the call came. It was Rich Bacus, National Products' EVP of manufacturing. He called to say congratulations and that they had selected High Beam for the production quality improvement project. Of course, I was literally shaking when he called, and I was just about speechless when he spoke the word "congratulations." I told him that on behalf of the entire High Beam organization we appreciated the opportunity and that we would absolutely deliver. He said he was confident that we would.

I asked about next steps. He said that we needed to schedule a meeting to discuss the details of the installation, get the contract completed, and plan for the kickoff. He said he was assigning Chet Gretzky as the project leader for the installation. He added that someone on John Fuller's staff in contracting would be getting in touch with us on the agreement. Finally, he said that we needed to schedule a meeting with their CTO, Mike O'Shea, to begin reviewing the technology and ERP integration. He said his assistant Ann Kane would be my resource for scheduling. He thanked me and hung up.

My Reaction

I just sat there for a while, disbelieving. How far we had come in such a short period of time! I thought about where we'd started. I thought about how incredible my team had been in supporting this deal. We'd knocked it out of the park and they were the reason why. I thought about how great it is to work for such an awesome company with such committed and talented people. Quality Brands didn't have a chance against us. We are the best. It affirmed my continued commitment to High Beam Industries. I have had some ups and downs with the company, I have had a few recruiters call, but on this day, at this point, I couldn't think of anything that could make me leave High Beam. And of course, I was in line for a very big payday!

The Celebration

The first call was of course to my husband, Richard. I told him that we'd won the National Products deal. He was thrilled. I think he was relieved, too, having had to live through all of the anxiety and stress that I'd taken home with me as I poured myself into this deal. But hey, we'll take a nice vacation and he'll just have to deal with it.

The next call I made was to Carl. He answered the phone and said, "Tell me something good", and I screamed, "We did it"! He yelled back, "Great job Susan, you really deserve this one. How exciting. I will let Ralph and Julie know. You are a star. Great job. Now, go take your husband out to dinner and have some champagne on High Beam." So I did!

....

Recognition—A New Award

This exchange took place between High Beam's Ralph Morris, EVP of sales, and Julie Moore, CEO, two days after hearing about the National Products win.

> *Julie: Review for me again the specifics of the National Products deal. I want to make sure I understand the financials of it.*

Ralph: It will be a three-year contract worth $12 million dollars. In year one, we'll bill National Products $8 million dollars. That includes over half of their spray gun conversions, services, and the installation of the software. In year two we'll bill them $3.5 million for the full conversion of all plants. The margin on this deal is tremendous. We will be making 32%, 4 points higher than our standard pricing for a large contract. Basically, this is the most profitable deal we have ever closed. In year three we'll bill them $500K for the ongoing maintenance program.

Julie: That is incredible. If only we could get the entire sales organization to sell this way. I know it's competitive out there, but this deal shows the whole company what is possible. It says clearly that when we focus on the value we deliver, we can win and be profitable doing it.

Ralph: We're working on that. It's part of our sales team development effort.

Julie: Like you said the other day, this was a heroic effort by Susan. I have an idea. Let's get with Human Resources and put together a new sales recognition program. To illuminate this success and the approach and outcomes that selling profit impact can deliver, I would like to start a new award. We'll call it "Profit Hero of the Year." In my mind, a Profit Hero doesn't just deliver profitability for customers. They also deliver greater profitably for our company by defending margins, competing on profit improvement, and leveraging more of our capabilities and services. A "win-win situation" as they say.

Ralph: I agree, that's a fabulous idea. We've been looking for a new kind of incentive. Also, we'll explore training options to support the kinds of skills Susan and others have in selling profit improvement.

Julie: I envision the criteria for the award would include the highest sales achieved, sales to quota, margin targets, and new customers. I want to also include a component that includes the aggregate profitability delivered to customers. This is critical to the message: When customers win, we win. We'll have to work with sales operations and finance to nail that down. I want to reward this type of selling. Plus, we need to include a financial reward with it. I mean, if the Profit Hero is successful, he or she will have earned an added bonus, and we'll be able to pay it.

Ralph: We should also have a companion award for the other team members in sales that help the team every day. One more thing I would add. How about with the Profit Hero of the Year Award we include "A Day with the CEO." We could have the winner work along with you and participate in staff meetings, phone calls, and executive meetings. It will elevate the idea that in being a Profit Hero you elevate yourself in the mind of your customers to the level of "peer." Besides, it will reinforce a key part of what we are trying to get our salespeople to do, which is "Think like executives." What better way than to hang out with the CEO and executive team? I think it would give the award a little extra excitement.

Julie: Excellent idea! Set up a meeting with HR to begin putting this together. Susan Stafford will be our first annual Profit Hero of the Year; we'll schedule her day with the leadership team next month.

Chapter 3

It's All about Profitability—How Customers Are Changing

"Rule No. 1: Never lose money.
Rule No. 2: Never forget Rule No. 1."
—*Warren Buffett*

I know from long experience that Quality Products still wins deals like the one it presented to National Products. Relationships do matter, and an installed base is leverage. Combined with documented cost savings, they make a winning formula. Yet what High Beam accomplished was significant for a couple of reasons. High Beam was able to get into the competition by getting to the C-level and grabbing the customer's attention thanks to a new and unique way of looking at their business. But what really changed the game for them was proving to National Products that doing business with High Beam would deliver significant profit improvement and be good for shareholders.

After all, that is what the executives at National Products ultimately care about, and the solution they bought did that through the profitability High Beam promised. They assessed the risks and rewards of making the large investment and then made the commitment based on the return on investment they believed they would achieve. High Beam made the case that it was a financial decision and not just an operational upgrade to National Products' manufacturing process. Best of all, High Beam won, too, by making it clear that the upgrade could help National Products dramatically grow their revenue and profitability in the process.

Customers are in a state of perpetual motion around growing revenue, managing costs and achieving a strong return on capital. That is their mission. Their reward is greater profitability and being able to send shareholders a fat dividend check. That's not new. What *is* new is the higher grade of enterprise-wide financial rigor and accountability being instilled at every level of the organization and in every division. Those things used to be reserved for the finance department and division heads who answered to senior management at budget time, but no longer.

The *New* New Economy

In the 1990s the technology boom helped create a new kind of economy. It was technology- and information-based, driven by low-cost capital, characterized by high-risk technology start-ups and a boom-and-bust mentality that made investors fearless. Fed Chairman Alan Greenspan called it "irrational exuberance" when the bubble burst in 2000. Then September 11 happened, opening investors' eyes to a new source of risk and adding a fear quotient. But what really sent us reeling was the financial meltdown in 2008 and the Great Recession that followed. It was painful for everyone, and we are still feeling the effects. Billions were lost in 401k's and stock portfolios. Job losses were high, and most have not come back. The banking meltdown made financing hard to find. Companies shelved their capital projects, cut costs, reduced inventories, and downsized workforces.

The consequences of those events are still playing out in our economy today. According to the *Wall Street Journal*,[1] in the eight recessions from the end of World War II through the end of the 1980s, the United States averaged about 20 months for employment to return to its pre-recession level. But after a relatively shallow

---

[1]   Ben Casselman, "Risk-Averse Culture Infects U.S. Workers, Entrepreneurs," *Wall Street Journal*, June 2, 2013.

recession in the early 1990s, it took 32 months for payrolls to replenish. After the even milder recession of 2001, it took four years.

As I write in 2014, four years after the end of the last recession, unemployment remains at historically high levels. Many economists attribute the trend to increased automation and outsourcing, which is allowing companies to produce more with fewer workers. Politicians tell us that slow economic growth of 2% to 3% and lower employment levels are a function of global trends toward a more balanced economy. We are told that this is the new economy, the "new normal." Instead of what used to be normal for this stage of a recovery (5% to 7% economic growth with unemployment below 5%), growth is only 1–2%, and unemployment still about 6%.

While most indicators are pointing up, don't bother telling that to business owners. It doesn't feel that way to them. Thanks to a slew of new financial regulations that many see as an over-reaction to the financial crisis, financing remains difficult to obtain for many businesses, and the reporting requirements have become incredibly burdensome for businesses of all sizes. Where in the past getting a loan to start or expand a business was fairly easy, today the threshold is so high that many companies give up before they start, go out of business, sell, or simply plod along at survival level.

Customer Behavior

Our current economic challenges have forced companies to do business in a different way. A new level of financial rigor has been created out of necessity. Fear and fiduciary responsibility have overtaken the more risk-tolerant and freewheeling style of running a business that we saw in the 1990s and part of the decade that followed. Before 2008, cash was always king for every business, but since then it's been elevated to a god. Too many companies were caught shorthanded, a situation that brought tremendous stress to CEOs and CFOs who relied on financing and strong cash flow to help fund their day-to-day operations and to execute their growth strategies.

To protect themselves in a stagnant economy, U.S. non- financial companies in 2012 filled their bank accounts with an additional $130 billion in cash, taking their total cash to a record $1.45 trillion.[2] Interestingly, in 2012 corporate revenues ticked up 2% to $11.1 trillion, while cash flow from operations remained flat at $1.4 trillion, yet corporate cash reserves grew 10%. That trend continued in 2013.

Building up that much cash usually indicates that corporate leaders are reacting to uncertainties, such as those caused by healthcare reform, changes in tax policy, and new financial and EPA regulations. That means companies are still sitting on the sidelines waiting for another shoe to drop. Their inactivity stalls the kind of forward planning and investment that salespeople need their customers to make if they are to grow their revenue. When too many unforeseen and uncontrollable external events happen, CEOs and CFOs hunker down, recalibrate risks, and demand greater management visibility and accountability for every economic decision made in their company. This has a serious ripple effect on employees and suppliers.

Ripple Effect

There continues to be a sharp focus on expense control, inventory management, speeding up receivables, and slowing down payables. Most discretionary spending is heavily constrained. To ensure visibility, control, and financial accountability, bigger decisions get pushed to higher levels of the organization. Take National Products, for example. The production team knew what needed to be done and had estimated the investment for the quality improvement project.

---

[2]   "U.S. Companies Stashing More Cash Abroad as Stockpiles Hit Record $1.45T," Forbes.com, March 19, 2013.

Operationally, they did their jobs and provided senior management with the details they needed to make the desired improvements and size the investment. They were, they believed, positioned to analyze need and empowered to drive the decision.

But they lacked an understanding of the big-picture financial strategies of the corporation's executive leadership: plans for capital investment, the focus on improved margins, and the drive for sustainable and profitable revenue growth. When the executives stepped in and took action, they dramatically expanded the scope and accelerated the project based on economics. Essentially, the compelling business case for improving profitability that High Beam made was one that the internal staff hadn't even attempted to make.

For employees, the pressure is greater than ever to justify every investment and expenditure in a way that supports the corporate financial goals. It usually manifests in not taking as many risks, focusing on price, and gathering a consensus around any decision that exceeds a certain level. For salespeople, that presents tremendous challenges, as they now have to navigate additional obstacles, such as their customers' desire to hold on to their cash.

A New Financial Culture

What salespeople are experiencing in many customer firms is the emergence of a new financial culture. I have spent 12 years helping CEOs and CFOs build the financial competencies of their employees and managers at every level of the organization. Educating the organization about how the company makes money is fundamental to sound decision making. Too often in the past, employees made decisions in their areas that were counter to the company's overall financial goals. Underutilized staff, expense control, leasing-versus-buy decisions, inventory levels out of balance with customer demand, and other actions that speed or impair cash flow all have a direct impact, positive or negative, on financial performance.

CEOs and CFOs are actively involved in building this financial culture. I have a client in the Midwest that deployed an enterprise-wide financial literacy program aimed at getting every employee, from the manufacturing plant's hourly employees all the way up to the leadership team, to understand clearly how their decisions influence financial performance. At the plant level it was about scrap, overtime, and safety, all of which had a direct impact on the plant's profitability. The CFO led every session, kicking if off with the company's financial management philosophies as a way of educating the organization about how they kept score, and about how cost- or capital-based decisions affect profit sharing and the overall health of the company. At every monthly management meeting, he made managers calculate their financial ratios (gross margins, operating expense ratios, operating ratios, cash flow) and had them report on how their departments or divisions were impacting financial results. This new insight helped everyone understand that the individual decisions they make all contribute to the company's bottom line.

CFOs have told me that one way to generate improved profitability is to have a workforce that understands that every dollar of cost they can avoid or eliminate drops right to operating profit. The organization can then begin to achieve greater awareness of and commitment to the strategies of the company, and everyone understands how they ultimately achieve salary increases, bonuses, and job security. Of course, it also puts every expenditure under a microscope. Where in the past discretionary spending allowed for freedom in making commitments, now the culture is around return on investment and profitability, which are often achieved through cost savings. Translation: lower prices and fewer suppliers.

Changing Centers of Influence

This laser focus on profitably is changing the centers of influence. At National Products the assumption was that the operational side of the organization was in control of the decision. They were the content experts, they knew the technical requirements, and they were in the best position to make the decision via a recommendation to the economic buyers. Yet when presented with a compelling financial business case that aligned with the executives' profit goals, the influence and the decision quickly shifted to the executive committee. That is a consequence of the new financial culture.

I hear regularly from salespeople that their greatest challenge is to understand how customers' buying influences are shifting. It can vary by company and by industry. Some companies are centralizing decisions and focusing heavily on lowest price as a cost management strategy. That has always been a challenge for salespeople, but today it has become a major problem. Take the healthcare industry. Because of the slow economy and the changes that the massive Affordable Care Act has had on the industry, many surgeons are no longer able to dictate which medical devices a hospital will buy. In the past, they were viewed as the experts, so procurement and hospital administrators complied because they needed the revenue and wanted to keep the surgeons happy. But as the economy has squeezed hospitals financially, and as the Affordable Care Act layers on additional financial burdens, hospital executives have taken more of the decision-making power out of the hands of practitioners and moved it to the administrators, who have the wider view of the entire enterprise.

Instead of selecting and purchasing a surgeon's medical device of preference, hospitals are using "value analysis" teams that include representatives of cross-functional areas, including finance, procurement, and supply chain, to compile a list of equally performing suppliers who can meet the technical, patient quality, and safety outcome requirements within their new cost parameters. Medical device companies have seen their entire marketplace upended by how hospitals are managing their business and making economic decisions. This is also true for many of the other manufacturers and suppliers that sell to healthcare. Another major trend is the explosion in outsourcing and reengineering of entire supply chains. Executives want more accountability, visibility, and control of all elements of their supply chain, from raw materials through manufacturing to delivery to the customer. That says that companies are continuing to look for new ways to lower costs, speed up cash flow, and reduce inventories to help them navigate the slow-growing economy. Growth solves a lot of problems; today's lack of it serves to rivet the organization on new or alternative profit improvement strategies for achieving their operating income targets.

Consensus Decision Making on Steroids

One consequence of a slow labor market is greater accountability for results. Combined with concerns about job security, it has led to an epidemic of consensus decision making. I find that department heads, as well as functional and divisional leaders, are deferring to committees to politically cover their bases and to ensure significant decisions are vetted without exposing them to professional or career risk. Because financial performance is so scrutinized, every decision to commit the organization to a project or initiative is heavily consensus-based. This spreads risks and insulates individuals from the spotlight of financial analysis.

For salespeople, this has become a major obstacle to the sales process. More than that, it typically lengthens the sales cycle, making it harder to close business in a timely fashion.

What's Your Profit IQ?

It is clear that customers are changing rapidly and that their focus is now heavily on return on investment and growing profitability. There is not a single decision made in your customer's business that isn't driven by economics. And C-level decision makers who are willing to spend time with salespeople want to know they are dealing with someone who understands their business and can deliver profitability. In short, they want to deal with businesspeople who have a high Profit IQ.

How do you measure your Profit IQ? Here are a few quick questions that will help you determine where you are in the eyes of a C-level executive. Regardless of your answers, your mission is to build your financial intelligence and ability to analyze your customer's business at a whole new level. After you take this Profit IQ test, the rest of the book is devoted to helping you raise your score.

1. **How much do you understand about your customer's business?**

   Executive-level decision makers want to deal with strong businesspeople. That means understanding how to analyze their business and understand, in financial, operational, and strategic terms, what they are doing and where they are going. You need to know:

   - The industry, the organization, and the business model
   - How they go to market
   - Industry trends
   - Key competitors
   - What differentiates them in the market
   - Key strategies for growth

2. **Do you know how your customers keep score?**

   Understanding how customers keep score requires understanding finance and knowing their industry, company-specific financial metrics, and the key performance ratios they use to measure profitability and return on investment. Customers expect you to know about:

   - Revenue growth (trends, challenges, opportunities)

- Gross margins and how they are performing against the market and key competitors
- Operating margins and implications for ongoing profitability
- Key financial metrics (EBITDA, operating expense ratios, return on assets)
- Asset management and their challenges (cash flow, inventory, accounts receivable, capital expenditures)

It is no longer enough to read an income statement and know if a company is making money. It is now about the interpretive value of the analysis you do in order to understand "how" customers manage the economics of their business.

3. How are your customers performing?

To access the C-suite and to build credibility, you need to know:

- Are they winning against their primary competitors?
- Are they growing faster than or as fast as the market is growing (gaining or losing market share)?
- Where is their growth coming from and how will they sustain it?
- How are they performing against Wall Street and shareholder expectations?
- What pressures are they under relative to their customer trends?
- And, if they are losing, what's the cause?
- What are the trends and what can they expect going forward?

4. What are they doing about their performance?

If a company is profitable and growing, their challenge is to sustain their success. If a company is challenged, it will be about making changes to turn things in the right direction. Regardless of their situation, they have usually put in place two or three key strategies and/or initiatives to address their business needs. These strategies come from the top, they are economically driven, and they have the attention of executive management. Moreover, they are funded and resourced to fulfill their mission. The first step in proving you can deliver profit improvement is understanding what financial and business strategies and initiatives they've chosen to achieve their goals.

5. **What can *you* do to improve your customer's performance?**

If you understand the customer's business, know their key profit drivers and their key strategies for improving profitability, then you are in a position to map your solutions to the specific areas that will bring the greatest impact for your customer. That is what being a Profit Hero is all about: making the connection and proving your profit impact.

The ultimate question you must be prepared to answer from an executive level decision maker is: *"How will doing business with you impact my profitability?"* Susan Stafford answered that question. You can, too.

Chapter 4

From Commoditization to Profit Impact— A Sales Transformation

---

"Courage is the power to let go of the familiar."
—*Raymond Lindquist*

I often hear salespeople and sales leaders lament that they are being commoditized by customers who focus only on price and unbundling the value of their solutions. They see this not only from procurement but also from operational, functional, and senior-level economic buyers. I hear the frustration from salespeople who work for highly differentiated companies with significant value engineered into their products, services, and delivery capabilities. They offer unique expertise and thought leadership in their respective industries, yet they get reduced to competing in lowest-price bake-offs that neutralize their competitive advantages.

Reasons Why Customers Commoditize Suppliers

Customers (buyers) tend to commoditize suppliers for three reasons. First, it is a cost management strategy. They know that one way to drive down their costs is to procure all services at the lowest price. It works! For every dollar of cost they can remove, that dollar drops directly to operating profit. Of course, it removes a dollar of operating profit for every supplier that participates.

Customers have installed business practices and incentives within their organizations to ensure that financial discipline and rigor are applied to every product or service acquisition. This leads to a lowest-cost mentality and a price-only culture. When customers seek to diminish your "value," it may be because they believe it's your way of extracting a higher price (supplier's margin) from each transaction at their expense. In short, it is their strategy for controlling the relationship and dictating the terms of doing business in a way that benefits their business.

Suppliers understand that in this exchange the total cost of doing business is not factored in, and in most cases it is more costly to do business based on price-only considerations. It is frustrating to know that although you are delivering tremendous results the customer is unwilling to recognize or reward you for the benefits you bring to their business. Of course, unless you completely understand the difference you bring and can articulate it, the battle wages on, you lose margin, and the customer "wins."

A second reason customers commoditize suppliers is because salespeople let them. If you can't defend your price by demonstrating the economic impact of your solutions, then you are destined to compete on price. Think about it: the constant in every product or service acquisition is the cost. It is not up to the customer to define the specific economic factors that impact their business as a result of deploying your solution. It takes time and effort to quantify the hard-dollar impact that your solution has on the customer's business. It is, frankly, the hardest part of selling profit impact. Take High Beam's Susan Stafford. She not only identified the specific ways she could affect National Products' business; she also quantified and positioned it in a way that demonstrated to the customer the specific financial drivers her solution affected, and ultimately the amount of profit improvement the customer would receive.

A third reason customers commoditize suppliers is to keep close track of how they are managing their supply chain. But in fact, when the focus is so narrowly defined around price, it becomes more difficult to leverage the total impact that a company offers. For example, consider a third-party logistics (3PL) and transportation company that provides services to thousands of customers. Shipping and transportation are in and of themselves highly competitive and driven by lowest-price decisions. They are volume-driven and highly transactional.

Over the years, the 3PL company has acquired and built technology solutions that can fully optimize the entire supply chain for a customer, providing visibility, lowest total cost shipping, and expertise for global forwarding, compliance, and other valuable services. They offer a significant level of overall profit improvement for an entire supply chain, from receiving supplier shipments to delivering finished products to customers.

Yet 3PLs often get into large bidding situations in which the customer wants quotes on a trucking-route-only basis (point A to point B). To the customer, this is a way to micro-manage transportation on a line-item basis and in a way that provides control and visibility into how they are managing their supply chain. For the supplier, it creates a quandary. Do they take a pass on significant transportation business, or do they compete and maybe win at less-than-desirable margins? The only other option is to take the opportunity to demonstrate that the customer's approach sub-optimizes their transportation spending overall and diminishes their profit improvement potential. That can be risky if the supplier doesn't make the business case. But the risk is even greater if they don't try.

Not every customer is focused on price only. Many sophisticated and forward-thinking executives understand that you get what you pay for, and that they can achieve better returns by allowing suppliers to have skin the game and make a profit as well. They lead companies that understand how to identify and evaluate economic return on investment. At least they are open to ideas and new ways of thinking about their business, and they will entertain suppliers who demonstrate knowledge of their business and can articulate how their solutions impact profitability. The problem is, even customers that operate on an economic impact basis will make a decision based on price if there isn't any other quantifiable way to evaluate an investment.

The Need for a New Sales Strategy

What all this means to salespeople is that the focus on price is not going away. There will always be a focus on price. There will always be competitors willing to sell on price. In fact, as the pressure to grow revenue increases, price as a selling strategy will become stronger. Companies that have a higher cost structure due to the added services and resources that accompany their solutions will feel pressure to defend profitable pricing more intensely than ever.

So how do you change the game and elevate your approach to a level that will allow you to compete on profit and win? The first salesperson who gets to an economic decision maker with a quantified, demonstrable profit improvement strategy will create a sustainable competitive advantage. What does a profit-centered sales approach look like? To answer that we first need to look at where selling is today.

How Sales Strategies Have Evolved

For companies that sell business-to-business, go-to-market sales strategies have evolved over time. They are created out of necessity in response to changing economic, customer, market, and competitive factors. Such factors include significant economic shifts like those we have experienced over the past several years; dynamic improvements in technology that change how and what customers buy; and innovation that spawns entirely new industries, new competitors, new market segments, or new ways of doing business. Look at how Apple has changed the landscape of business. The company has created entirely new product categories for which there are millions of new customers globally, with impact on all levels of the supply chain from component manufacturers to retail sales support organizations. And their iPad technology has now become a major player in corporate communication and information management.

Over the past 30 years, we have seen three major shifts in selling strategy. Each built on the one before it, addressing the business and competitive conditions encountered. In every case, sales strategies were engineered to address an organization's need to grow profitably. There has never been more pressure on profitable growth than there is right now. A slow-growing economy and increased competition fuel the need to get the upper hand in acquiring and retaining customers. For each new strategy designed to address the need to win in the market, there are early adopters who usually have a head start and set the mark. The followers are forced to change because customers begin to drive change through their buying behavior.

Strategy One: Product-Centered Selling

It is natural that the earliest sales strategies were rooted in product or service differentiation. The focus was on features and benefits, how the products performed, and how they compared with competitors'. Any new product introduced to the market today has about six months before competitors replicate and even surpass its capabilities. When that occurs, the market recognizes that the only thing differentiating companies and their products is their price. Soon the battle is all about growing and retaining market share by driving greater volume through larger quantity purchasing. This leads to national agreements or contracts based on price and volume. Customers assert their buying power by dangling the volume card, and most product- and price-driven suppliers take the bait.

From a relationship standpoint, companies that compete on product and price are viewed as vendors, and the key drivers to the relationship are price and availability. It is all about delivering the right product, in the right quantities, at the right time, and at the right price. If that doesn't happen, there are competitors lined up to take their place. A supplier's behavior usually becomes reactive, with survival as the desired business outcome. For a company to thrive with a product-centered sales strategy, it must be committed to being the most efficient, lean, and low-cost player in the market. The common characteristic of these kinds of companies is typically a single or limited product offering that is able to win through product superiority, performance, availability, supply chain reliability, and of course, price.

Strategy Two: Solution-Centered Selling

This strategy was born out of the frustration of suppliers realizing that the price/volume game is a losing proposition. As they made more and more investments to enhance the product or service offering, they found it harder to get a return; competing on product and price was a zero-sum game. When the smarter companies stood back and looked at it, they realized that they were providing a great deal of operational or business improvement. This often included the superior performance of their products and services, their unique industry expertise, and the problem solving they provided to customers. There had to be a better way of winning business. Providing customers with a bundled solution seemed the way to best leverage their full capabilities. Many companies positioned it as a "total systems" approach.

This accomplished a couple things. First, it allowed a supplier to differentiate on more of an operational basis—that is, by defining the purchase in ways that included other operational elements and not in product-only terms. For example, consider a supplier that is in the business of providing a product that has hazardous materials as part of its construction, which must be properly handled before, during, and after installation. The supplier may include installation by a specialist and disposal of the replaced product in compliance with federal guidelines, releasing the customer from liability. They might eliminate the need for the customer to have specialists in-house, which will reduce labor. They might also include regular maintenance by a trained technician and a warranty service. These companies focus on "total systems" thinking and how their product or services actually affect a customer's ability to operate at an optimum level. They want to be viewed as ones that can be counted on.

The approach typically includes bundling products and services to provide greater leverage and operational efficiencies—fewer suppliers to deal with, fewer SKUs to manage, fewer employee hours spent maintaining multiple systems. They differentiate themselves by showing how acquiring products and services as a total solution is a more economical and lower-cost way of doing business. Of course, this strategy is designed to grow revenue while protecting margins by bundling products, service, and pricing. One of the benefits of Solution-Centered Selling is that it allows suppliers to put the customer's decision more in the context of operational and technical factors and less in the realm of itemizing product price.

Strategy Three: Value-Centered Selling

The problem with Solution-Centered Selling is that competitors and customers have figured it out. It has come full circle. As more procurement-savvy companies begin to analyze the financials of their entire supply chain, looking for efficiencies and cost take-out, they have begun to unbundle solutions. They cherry pick and then price-compare components. With better information they are now holding suppliers accountable for all the costs associated with a "total solution." As buying influence gets more centralized and procurement takes on more control, selling solutions to operational levels left companies competing on price. Only now, there are more services included that suppliers are not being paid for, nor are they necessarily getting credit for providing them. In fact, one of the biggest frustrations of sales executives is that their companies have invested heavily in the systems and services that help them differentiate their solutions and now those investments (real costs that impact their margins) are becoming nothing more than table stakes. So we are back to a price battle with even less profit margin to go around.

In response, companies realized they were dealing with the wrong people. If the decisions are moving from operational levels to a more centralized procurement process, and if the focus is even more intensely on price, then the only way to succeed is to get to the economic decision makers who will ultimately have an interest in the impact a supplier can deliver to their business. Value-Centered Selling emerged as a way to redefine what they were buying and by doing so elevate the discussion to an economic one.

As a result, today's dominant sales strategy is Value-Centered Selling. There is not a day that goes by that I don't see the word "value" applied to some aspect of what someone is selling: "We provide value-added products and services." "We deliver greater economic value, the value of doing business with us is . . ." But how is that value defined? That is the key. Selling value is a way of elevating Solution-Centered Selling by quantifying the payback on a specific opportunity. Typically, value is a term used to win business, defend higher price, and identify a specific set of qualities that help set a company and their products and services apart from competitors. I see it as opportunistic.

There is nothing wrong with this approach, and while salespeople are able to get to higher-level economic buyers, it often comes down to a situational sale. The goal is to become a partner to the customer and be in a position to expand the level of business with fewer competitive challenges. Most companies I work with tend to identify an opportunity or situation, whether big or very specific (a new medical device and procedure, a new software upgrade, outsourcing a specific function). The focus is on payback, usually in the form of quantified cost savings.

Most value-based proposals I see focus on the immediate payback of the purchase being made. Some do it well, others can't offer a hard-dollar number that they are willing to defend. They often rely on factors outside the scope of the deal, and their claims ultimately become anecdotal. Over time, economic decision makers see through these tactics. That is why customers are demanding that suppliers articulate specifically how their proposals will impact profitability. Cost savings is not differentiation; everyone does it. Differentiation is in the interpretation and the ability to map economic outcomes based on what the customer is most concerned about.

In Value-Centered Selling, the goal from a relationship standpoint is to become a preferred supplier, one that has access to the C-suite and who can compete while their competitors are selling solutions and product/service capabilities to the procurement and operations levels. But I now see value selling being neutralized as the meaning of value gets diluted competitively and doesn't carry as much weight with economic buyers. In a lot of ways value has become commoditized. The market is moving rapidly toward profit improvement, and the buying criteria are becoming more and more influenced by the hard-dollar profit impact of every investment a customer makes.

The New Sales Strategy: Profit-Centered Selling

It was inevitable that it would come to this. If you can't compete on product and price, if your total solutions approach can be duplicated, and if selling value is not providing organizational or executive-level leverage, then competing on profit is the only way to achieve a competitive advantage. That is what High Beam's Susan Stafford learned. She proved that differentiation starts with selling to the right level, while positioning economic impact in a way that addresses the customer's changing financial needs and goals. She won National Products' business by quantifying her solution and delivering $27 million in improved profitability, not just for that initiative but for the corporation. She had the big picture in mind.

Profit-centered selling is no longer optional; it is how business must be done today. Customers are under unprecedented pressure to grow profitable revenue, lower costs, and utilize their assets effectively. In their minds there are only two types of salespeople: those who sell products or services and those who deliver profit improvement. Salespeople who sell their stuff are relegated to the procurement and operational levels. Salespeople who sell profit improvement are invited to participate on an ongoing basis in helping customers anticipate, plan, and execute their business plans successfully. Those who achieve this level will become peers and earnings contributors; they will own the customer relationship; and they will earn virtual immunity from competition. And if salespeople focus on selling and delivering profit improvement, they will do so not only for the customer but also for their own company, which is under the same pressure to grow their business profitably. In short, they will become Profit Heroes.

SALES STRATEGY EVOLUTION
Driven by new economic realities

Sales Strategy	Product-Centered Selling	Solution-Centered Selling	Value-Centered Selling	Profit-Centered Selling
Differentiation	Product/Price	Product/Service Bundling	Opportunity Payback	Customer Profitability
Role	Product Expert	Operational Expert	Business Problem Solver	Earnings Contributor
Relationship	Vendor	Valued Supplier	Preferred Supplier	Peer
Business Outcomes	Survival	Remain a Player	Stay Relevant	Own the Relationship

Chapter 5

The Profit-Centered Selling Process

"Give me a place to stand, and I will move the world."
—Archimedes

Susan Stafford is not the world's first Profit Hero. There are many salespeople who focus on customer profitability. They sell the new way; they have learned through trial and error how to identify, quantify, and sell profit improvement. They have experienced the exhilaration of winning business knowing that they beat their competitors on the biggest stage of all, at the top. They get a sense of satisfaction when they are able to lock down a deal knowing that their customer will experience significant profit improvement. They feel empowered to be even bolder and more confident with customers, confident that they can win any deal against competitors who continue to focus on their products and services.

But many other salespeople, who know that they deliver significant financial impact, face an obstacle: getting access to the C-suite to make their case. There is a massive traffic jam outside the executive suite because every organization on the planet has figured out that selling to the floors below is slow, costly, frustrating, and punishing. Of course, the ones that beat the traffic are those who have a story the executives want to hear; they are speaking the language of growth and profitability.

There are also those salespeople who work hard and hope their good intentions, hard work, high level of service, and operational impact pave the way upstream. Even though they attempt to reach higher levels, including the C-suite, they are often treated like "vendors." Bless those salespeople who believe in their solution so strongly that they just keep pounding away, battling it out in the trenches. Perseverance does pay off, but these days it takes more than being tenacious. It takes a process—a playbook that can be learned and applied.

I am often asked, "How can a salesperson deploy an effective profit-centered sales process that is repeatable, scalable, and sustainable?" Susan Stafford had a process. That process elevated her to the executive level with a powerful story about growth and profitability. I have mapped it out for you. If you leverage Susan's process, you too can achieve breakthrough success as a profit-centered salesperson.

THE PROFIT-CENTERED SELLING PROCESS

Learn	Align	Engage		Achieve
Discovery	Insight	Access	Execute	Prove
Financial & Business Analysis	Thought Leadership & Dollarization	C-Suite & Economic Decision Makers	Sell & Deploy Profit Improvement	Track, Measure & Document Results

Learn

The first phase of Susan's profit improvement sales process is learning. Building customer intelligence is more than building a basic account profile or understanding the demographics of the company, although all that is important. It is now about building three kinds of knowledge: *operational knowledge, organizational knowledge, and financial knowledge.* All three are important, but at the end of the day, understanding the key financial drivers that are guiding customers' decisions will be the most important information you will need in building and delivering a profit improvement solution.

The Discovery Process

Susan knew going in that she was behind the 8-ball. She had only been in the account for 60 days, and she didn't have the kinds of relationships with National Products that could provide her in-depth knowledge of the company, operations, people, and politics. Her competitor Vince Billings had spent five years cultivating a network within the company that fed him information and other news about key changes and kept him connected to the business. He had control of the account.

So she believed step one was to accelerate her knowledge of National Products, especially the factors that would provide her leverage with executives. She knew that her best shot was to get to the economic decision makers and sell them on a game-changing idea. She deployed a discovery process aimed at understanding the financial, operational, and performance drivers that her solution would need to address for her to be successful. And she began identifying the areas she needed to connect to help the customer understand how her solution would drive profitability.

Learn about Your Customers' Business

Discovery starts with understanding your customers' business, their industry, markets, customers, and competition. It is important to know how they are performing and what they are doing to improve their business results. Learning about customers goes beyond profiling the organizational structure and how they segment their business. It now takes understanding the roles and backgrounds of the key decision makers, where they came from, and how they might have been influenced in their careers. For instance, I run into a lot of executives who spent time at General Electric. They approach business in a unique fashion, and most are hired because of their experience with a high-profile company.

There is not a day that goes by that I don't learn about a new website, a new application, a "just-released" device, or an enhancement that adds speed and reach to how we communicate. It seems as though everything you ever wanted to know is literally at your fingertips. That sounds great, but what happens when it gets in the way of doing business? The fact is, all of these innovations and enablers are speeding up change to a pace most of us have never experienced and are ill-prepared for. The faster and more sophisticated our technology-driven workplace gets, the more we need to know how to distill, internalize, and integrate these business enablers into daily sales and communication practices that allow us to be successful. What is the impact of some of these changes? The entire relationship with a customer may now hinge on how well a salesperson can access information and apply it to solving customer business and financial problems—and do it faster and better than the competition.

The Role of Technology and Social Networking

You can't talk about social networking without addressing the explosion of data over the past five years. You don't have to look any further than your smart phone for the impact speed has had on technology. Smart phones have always been on a 12-month innovation cycle for features and device capabilities. What has changed is the massive integration of data, applications, communication, and sharing. You can quickly find a company, its address, and a contact, and your phone's GPS will take you to their doorstep. As more and more companies trust, embrace, and invest in cloud computing, the mobility and flexibility will only accelerate.

Accelerating Customer Knowledge

For salespeople, gaining access to the right people and building customer relationships continue to be major success factors. But how to get there, and most of all, *what* to do when you get there not only defines success but may define an entire career.

Today information about a customer's organizational structure and decision makers is at your fingertips, literally, thanks to websites like LinkedIn, Hoovers.com, Data.com (formerly Jigsaw), and Zoominfo.com. Many of these websites allow you to search by title, function, department, geography, and more. Learning the backgrounds of key contacts is possible. In fact, today chances are you have a savvy competitor who has done his due diligence the night before on his laptop at his kitchen table. He knows the college your customer attended and that he was a Phi Kappa Sigma. He knows he has two kids and their approximate ages. He may have learned that the customer's son was the high school starting quarterback and was recruited by State University.

He probably learned that the customer was recently promoted, has three conference presentations on YouTube espousing his company's thought leadership in the market, and has two white papers on a highly regarded association website. He probably hit LinkedIn and found five people he knew that are first-level contacts with the customer, and learned that one of them had written a recommendation on his profile. One quick phone call and your competitor now has a personal connection and information that a highly networked and inquisitive salesperson might have. Of course, it's important to avoid giving the impression that you "know" an executive just because you discovered information about him or her on LinkedIn or YouTube, but these sites are nevertheless an important source of information.

Then he turned his attention to the customer's website and dug into its financials, 10-K, executive presentations, and recent press releases. In analyzing the financials, he learned of their strategy to address their profitability slide, including their plans to lower operating costs. He knows how they are "spinning" their financial performance to the shareholders. And in fact, during the last earnings call, John Smith from Oppenheimer had asked the

CEO what the expected financial return was on the $300 million marketing campaign your competitor believed he had a solution for.

Finally, he was able to compile all of this information into a set of talking points and line of questioning that shows him to be one of the most informed and engaged salespeople the customer has ever met . . . and all of that on a first call!

With the economic pressures customers are experiencing and with the speed and reach that information and technology are providing, the interpretive value of the data and what you do with the information are key, regardless of where you get it. In short, can you turn data into knowledge and leverage that into actionable outcomes?

Align

The second phase is aligning with the organization, and especially with the executives you hope to engage. Once you are equipped with an in-depth understanding of the customer's business, the next step is to provide thought leadership—new information or ideas about how they can manage their business more effectively. CEOs are paid to look ahead; it is their job to understand where the market is going, how their company is performing relative to customer trends and demand, competitors, economic, and global issues.

CEOs pay a lot of people within the organization to be expert at what they do. But they also know that there are limitations to being inside an organization, insulated from external changes and trends. That is why many salespeople are successful in differentiating their companies by providing thought leadership, a strong position on a way of doing business or solving problems. It is usually based on experience or research and is usually in support of the business case they are making for investing in their business. For salespeople, leveraging your company's thought leadership and research is a way of redefining a customer problem for which a profit-driven solution can be made available in a way that aligns with an organization and demonstrates a business fit.

Susan did an effective job of analyzing National Products' business, and not just from the financial standpoint. She knew that their production quality project was aimed at improving specific financial outcomes. In her analysis, she determined that there was a heavy emphasis on technology and having better decision support reporting throughout their production management system. Once she established that as a key driver for the CFO, she was able to leverage High Beam's research and thought leadership on the subject. It turned out to be the differentiator when she built her profit improvement strategy for National Products.

Engage

The third phase is about getting to the decision makers. Engaging economic decision makers is now more difficult than it's ever been. There are many obstacles to reaching the people who have the greatest interest in your solution. It would have been easier for Susan to spend her time nurturing relationships with the production level. Of course, even had she taken that approach, time was not on her side. Even if she was excellent at one-on-one relationship building, she would have been working against a lot of inertia and an embedded competitor. She saw engaging the CFO as her best shot at getting into the game.

When I work with salespeople who want to take their profit improvement solution to a C-level decision maker, the biggest challenge they face is getting access to the CEO, CFO, or other economic-level buyer. One CFO told me he had trained his assistant to defer and deflect or refer the hundreds of solicitations he receives from all types of salespeople and companies. It would have been nearly impossible to hear them all and attempt to identify the suppliers or ideas that warrant his time.

Achieve

Susan sold the deal to National Products based on the profit improvement she would deliver. But she also established, as part of the installation of the project, a communications strategy to ensure that all of the stakeholders were included in the retrofitting phase of the project. She had a documented process that she used with the executives. She not only got them to sign off on a stepped approach for the operational deployment but also sought and received a commitment from National's executives on the specific things they would track, measure, and report on.

Too many organizations that sell economic impact and are successful at persuading decision makers to buy their services come up short on institutional follow-through, which then gets diluted or goes undocumented. After a solution has been deployed and is operating, it is extremely difficult to review and reestablish all of the variables that you need to manage or control to get a realistic measurement of results.

Susan worked closing with the installation team, which included Chet Gretzky, National Products' director of manufacturing operations, to ensure she got the accountability and support she needed by creating a very visible set of interventions with production leadership, financial management, and executive leadership.

The final step in the profit-centered sales process is proving that what you sold in fact achieved the results you promised. Holding companies accountable for promised results is important to buyers today. Decision makers have become skeptical and weary of promises made by salespeople that too often never get followed up on or measured. By putting in the measurements and mechanisms for tracking results, Susan was able to go back at regular intervals to demonstrate how the needle was moving based on their mutual commitment and expectations for improved profitability.

Chapter 6

Learn

Customer Discovery and Financial Analysis

*"Give me six hours to chop down a tree and
I will spend the first four sharpening the axe."*
—*Abraham Lincoln*

Susan Stafford's approach started with a discovery process that helped her understand the customer's business and key profit goals. Information is power, and the more you know about your customer's business, their financial performance, profit improvement strategies, and key initiatives, the better position you will be in to align with them. This makes sense; everyone aspires to do it. However, what is the right information, and how do you find, access, and use it in a way that helps differentiate you from your competitors?

In the past, the art of selling was to get to the right people, ask the right questions, and get better intelligence. If I could get better information—personal insights my competitors didn't have and might not be able to get—I would have a significant competitive advantage. In a sense, having superior information created barriers to entry. Each and every interaction gave me leverage my competitor didn't have. I felt special if I had the customer's email and direct line. I was golden. Now, not so much. The questions and the information required revolve around a customer's financial performance and what you would do to impact their profitability.

The Right Information

Why does having the right information matter? It matters because, with nearly unlimited access to information, everyone can be on equal footing if they try. Hundreds of websites aggregate data on companies; social media give you the ability to find and connect with people that in the past you would have had a hard time even knowing about. Now, the challenge is to be the better analyst, the better technologist, the better communicator, the better networker, and the faster aggregator of data and well-sourced information. And it is no longer just about having demographic information or understanding the operational environment or the company's P&L. It is now about interpreting the *right* information in a new and different way.

If you are going to compete and win on profit, you need to look at the customer's business the way the customer looks at it. You need to think like the executive team. What are they looking at, what matters to them, and how can you tie your solutions to the economic drivers that get their attention? Customers expect you to know a lot about their business. Gone are the days that you can say to an executive *"Tell me about your business."* I'm pretty sure if you did that today you would be escorted out of the building.

Today executives expect you to understand trends in their business. From a financial standpoint, are they growing profitably and what is contributing to their success? How can they sustain it? They expect you to know the challenges they are facing related to customer demands, competition, and regulatory issues and how they impact margins. They want to deal with a businessperson who is able to identify areas in the supply chain that can be improved and drive stronger cash flow through better use of their working capital. They want to know that if they take the time to meet with a salesperson, that salesperson has insight that is valuable to the company in executing its strategic plan. What are the industry leaders doing? What are competitors doing? Of course this brings little comfort to many salespeople who don't have the time, inclination, or wherewithal to garner that much information.

It Starts with Financial Competence

You can't sell profit improvement without a strong understanding of finance. Financial literacy is fast becoming a core competency for salespeople who want to sell to higher levels and avoid competing on price. Being a strong businessperson allows you to engage executive level decision makers in a financial conversation about their business in a way that gets their attention, builds creditability, and focuses on areas the customer is most concerned with. There is not a decision made today in your customer's organization that isn't driven by economics. So understanding what the economic drivers are is foundational to profit-centered selling.

Building financial competency takes a concerted effort. Most salespeople get into sales for the competition, to work closely with customers, and to make money. Most don't get into sales to be a financial or business analyst. Salespeople are typically trained on their products and services, provided industry and competitive knowledge, and given the tools to win by differentiating what they sell. Most don't want to sit at a desk grinding through financial statements.

That hasn't changed. What has changed is that selling now requires the ability to discern what is happening in a customer's company from a business and financial standpoint, to understand how they are changing and what they are doing to address their business challenges. Translating these kinds of business issues helps you translate business intelligence into opportunity. Ultimately that is how you create new demand for your products and services in this new economic climate.

Let's face it, finance in some form has been around for thousands of years. Corporate finance today has become a real science, but for salespeople and what they need to know, it can be made easy to understand. In the end though, it's what you do with the information that is most important.

Keeping It Simple—What You Need to Know

I have worked with many Fortune 500 companies in building the financial competencies of their employees and sales organization. The goals for most are to build the skills to analyze a customer's business so that they can identify the business, operational, and financial issues that their solutions can address, then find areas of opportunity where they can make a difference, and finally quantify the specific hard-dollar ways they can deliver profit improvement.

1. Grow the Business

Every company is under increasing pressure to grow their business. Under Wall Street's watchful eye, CEOs are working hard to find ways to grow in an economy with strong headwinds. They might be focused acquisitions to expand their market potential and to leverage their scale in the marketplace. They might be introducing new products, growing market share, winning new customers, retaining and expanding existing customers, investing in marketing, and adding salespeople. Growing a business today usually means taking business away from competitors.

The question is, do you help customers grow their business? Do you help them go to market faster, provide a product or service that helps them be more competitive? I find many companies believe their solutions are aimed at "managing the business more efficiently" and focus more on cost take-out. But those who can show measurable impact on revenue generation have a tremendous opportunity to get executive attention, as growing revenue is the biggest challenge CEOs are facing today. There are a number of strategies that companies use to address revenue growth. The following are some of the areas that you can impact with your products or services:

- Acquisitions/mergers
- Advertising

- Marketing campaigns
- New products
- Sales force expansion
- New market segments
- Customer expansion
- Customer retention
- New customer acquisition
- New markets
- Price increases
- Global expansion

2. Manage Costs

Growing the business is a good thing if it is done profitably. That means managing costs including cost of goods sold (COGS—the direct costs attributable to production, as well as the materials and direct labor costs used to produce a good), and operating expenses (often called SG&A—sales, general, and administrative costs including sales, marketing, HR, technology, legal and other overhead). One of the reasons selling is so challenging today is that as economic growth lumbers along and companies grow at slower rates, the most effective way to generate consistent profitability is through tight fiscal controls. Companies must try to do more with less and find ways to be more productive with fewer resources. This is one of the main drivers of customers' new financial culture that is so heavily focused on cost management.

It is important to ask yourself whether your product or service directly impacts the customer's ability to manage costs. Does your software speed up workflow, thereby reducing labor costs? Do you lower operating costs by providing high-efficiency equipment? To get to profitability you must connect your solutions to the customer's key cost drivers. If you do, you are in a position to deliver profit improvement. There are a number of strategies that companies use to manage costs. Your products and services might improve your customers' performance in the following ways:

Cost of goods sold

- Lean manufacturing
- Lower raw materials costs
- Automation
- Improve quality
- Reduce the number of vendors

Operating expenses (SG&A)

- Labor cost reductions
- Reduce the number of vendors
- Reduce SKUs
- Manage travel expenses
- Streamline operations

3. Utilize Assets

To think like a CEO or CFO it is important to understand the balance sheet and how companies manage the capital invested in their business. Companies receive capital from investors and the bank in the form of loans, which support the company's infrastructure. Every investor wants to know that the CEO is achieving a strong return on their investment. The balance sheet is made up of assets and liabilities. Assets are broken into two categories, *current assets* and *fixed assets*. Depending upon the industry or business, most companies have a lot of money tied up in inventory, accounts receivables, warehouses, manufacturing facilities, and equipment.

Current assets include any asset that can be converted to cash within 12 months. This includes inventory and accounts receivable. It also includes cash on hand, which has been a major focus area for most companies. Having strong cash flow provides companies with options in deciding how best to invest in their business to grow and succeed in the market. The money tied up in accounts receivables has become a challenge as customers are slowing down payments in order to hang on to their cash longer.

Fixed assets are all of the facilities, warehouses, office space and equipment used to produce the company's products and services. Whether and when to invest, upgrade, or expand their fixed are ongoing questions for executive management.

Liabilities includes accounts payable and loans. Most CEOs would like their companies to get more out of the assets they currently have before investing in more. We have seen a great deal more of that in recent years as companies have held onto their cash. They would prefer to hold off capital expenditures as long as possible until there is greater certainty in the economy and in the market. When they do consider capital expenditures, it always comes down to three determining factors: Will this investment help me (1) grow revenue; (2) lower costs; (3) become more efficient?

Most companies I work with all impact current assets. It might be through solutions that speed up the use of inventory or reduce inventory on hand. In other cases it might be services that help customers speed up their supply chain and create a better environment for collecting receivables. If you sell solutions that require a capital expenditures, the question you have to answer is, do you help your customers better manage or utilize their assets? Can you help them reduce inventory, speed up accounts receivable, or improve the performance of their assets, such as their production facilities or equipment? There are a number of strategies that companies use to better manage assets. Your products and services might improve your customers' performance in the following ways:

Current Assets

- Reduce inventory
- Speed up receivables
- Increase automation
- Rationalize SKUs

Fixed Assets

- Lease versus buy
- Consolidate warehouses
- Manage travel expenses
- Sell or expand facilities

4. Achieve a Strong Return on Assets (ROA)

This is what executives get measured on. Basically, ROA is what shareholders can earn as a result of investing in a company. It might also be expressed as return on invested capital (ROIC). Or return on capital employed (ROCE), or return on investment (ROI). Regardless, it is a number executives manage closely. If you help a company grow revenue, manage costs, or get better use of their assets, then you are in a position to impact operating profit and ROA. ROA is calculated like this:

$$Operating\ Profit \div Total\ Assets\ (Current + Fixed\ Assets) = Return\ on\ Assets$$

Susan Stafford says:
My Financial Analysis of National Products

I don't do a deep dive on every customer or opportunity. I simply don't have the time. I have to pick my spots. If a customer like National Products has significant potential, I use a simple but structured approach to gather the information I need to position my company and solution as a profit improvement strategy. I always start my discovery process by looking at the customer's financials.

You can't sell profit improvement if you don't know how the customer keeps score. After all, this is what the relationship is all about, my ability to directly connect my solutions to their key economic drivers and profitability. I have learned that you don't need to be a CPA to understand business finance. You don't have to be a CFO or come from a financial background to understand how your customers manage their financials. Some salespeople have been exposed to accounting, and some have had jobs where they have had to deal with finance. But most don't deal with finance on a daily basis. It has simply not been a part of the job description—at least up to now. The fact is, the key to success in the future is being able to diagnose the financial performance of a company just like a doctor studies all of a person's vitals before prescribing a remedy.

I learned early on that no matter what you sell, you primarily deal with a customer's operating performance. You impact their operations. You might sell spray guns, software, transportation services, banking services, insurance, building maintenance, a medical device, commodity-based raw materials or highly engineered products. In the end what you do assists customers in better managing their business and executing their profit strategies. So for me, it is all about the key metrics that tell me how well they are operating the company. With that in mind, I have a simple way of analyzing customer financials. I break it down in the following way.

Growth and Profitability

To learn how a company is performing, look at the trend and see what they are doing about it. They are either growing profitably and need to sustain their growth. Or they are not growing at their desired pace and are deploying strategies to improve their performance. Sustainable profit growth drives a company's ability to expand the business and to invest in ways that will continue that growth. Investors want to invest in growth companies that are profitable year after year and continue to deliver shareholder returns. So I want to know the following:

- Are they growing profitably?
- Are they winning against their key competitors?

- Are they investing in the business?
- Are they expanding or acquiring?
- Are they getting a return for shareholders?
- Are they in pain?

The Scorecard (Typical Income Statement)

This can vary by industry, but I find that most industries follow a financial model similar to the one below:

	Revenue
-	**Cost of Goods Sold (COGS)**
=	**Gross Profit**
	Gross Profit Margin % (Gross Profit ÷ Revenue)
-	**Operating Expenses**
	Operating Expense Ratio (Operating Expense ÷ Revenue)
=	**Operating Profit**
	Operating Profit Margin % (Operating Profit ÷ Revenue)

A couple of years ago I asked my stock broker, Brent Casey, how he looks at companies when he is considering investments. I thought if he were challenging CEOs and CFOs to justify their business performance, then there was something I could learn from how he approaches his research. He gave me a chart he uses to explain the key financial areas to nonfinancial colleagues at his firm.

Metric	Definition	Why It's Important
Revenue	Finished products and/or services sold to customers, through distribution or products sold to OEMs	To know how they go to market; who their customers and competitors are
COGS (cost of goods sold)	Direct costs attributable to the production of goods. Includes costs of materials along with the direct labor costs used to produce the goods	Is the first expense executives look at in determining the productivity of their business
Gross Profit	The financial metric used to assess a firm's financial health—gross profit is the money left over from revenues after cost of goods sold	Tells you how well the company is competing in the market
Gross Profit Margin Percent	Gross Profit ÷ Revenue	Shows the trend of how effective a company is over time
Operating Expenses	Sales, general & administrative expenses—salaries, commissions, marketing, R&D, HR, legal, travel, sales, and advertising expenses a company incurs.	Tells you how many resources were used to produce a dollar of revenue

Operating Expense Ratio Percent	Operating Expense ÷ Revenue	An important efficiency ratio of how well a company is managing its internal and external resources
Operating Profit	The profit achieved after all expenses. Basically, how much money the business made operationally	A measure of how well they are running the business.
Operating Profit Margin Percent	Operating Profit ÷ Revenue	Shows the trend of how profitable a company is over time

Brent said he first looks at a company's "growth profile." That includes the top line or *revenue*. He explained that he wants to know whether a company is growing revenue and winning in the market. In other words, is it growing faster than or as fast as the market? Other things he asks about in his growth profile are:

- Is the company's growth organic, or is it achieved through acquisition or mergers?
- Is the company growing through new product innovation and expanding its market potential as a result? Expanding market potential would indicate strong future growth.
- Or is the company in a mature industry where it's simply trying to maintain or defend market share?

All of these questions were certainly appropriate for me to ask National Products. I knew from my research that they were barely growing. That was going to take some additional digging. For Brent, knowing a company's growth profile gave him insights into their viability as a potential investment. For me, it would mean knowing what the challenges were and what the opportunities for growth were that I could impact. If I am going to sell profit improvement, I need to know what overriding business issues executive management will be focused on.

National Products' *Revenue*

Using Brent's growth profile, I took a look at National Products' profile before my meeting with the CFO John Fuller. I saw a company in pain.

Fiscal Year	2012	% Change	2011	2010
Revenue	$9.75B	+1%	$9.67B	$9.77B

While revenues were up, they were only up 1%, although I had read that National had forecast 7%–10%. That was a big shortfall. So I asked John Fuller about it: *"I noticed that you missed your revenue forecast last year, What were some of the reasons for that?"*

John's answers:

- We lost revenue to the big-box retailers due to missed shipments.
- We experienced higher-than-normal product returns due to quality issues, and that revenue was not recovered.
- Competitors' deep discounting in key seasonal periods resulted in lost business and lost margin.
- Supply inefficiencies due to the lack of visibility into our shipment problems were costly, especially with key customers.
- Our new revenue from the Water Filtration Division was slower to ramp up than expected, which led to lower sales.

I knew that I would need to get specific answers to the questions, things like the actual dollar amount of revenue lost to the big-box retailers and what the normal returns were without the problems.

I also noticed that nowhere in the RFI or production quality audit did National Products address lost revenue, even though their revenue trend was down. I saw that as a major differentiator if I could quantify the economic impact that our solution could deliver around growing revenue.

National Products' *Cost of Goods Sold*

Next I looked at COGS. From the start I suspected that the production quality improvement audit and initiative were aimed squarely at impacting COGS. I see that a lot with organizations that want to deploy Six Sigma projects. What I found was not a pretty picture:

Fiscal Year	2012	% Change	2011	2010
COGS	$6.71B	+3.4%	$6.49B	$6.45B

COGS was up 3.4%, meaning that something was going on with production. It was raw materials, productivity, or some other factor. My hunch was that the company's COGS increases made their Production Quality Improvement Initiative even more urgent. National Products wanted to:

1. Increase product throughput by 5%
2. Reduce defects and/or re-finishing rates by 5%
3. Reduce production downtime due to maintenance and repairs by 10%
4. Improve energy efficiency to meet corporate sustainability goals
5. Improve maintenance monitoring and reporting

I am 100% certain that their production quality audit found that they needed to upgrade and retrofit their outdated and inefficient spray gun systems. COGS is a huge area of opportunity for our spray gun systems, but also, a picture was emerging that our Intelligent Monitor software could play a direct role in speeding up production throughput and reducing defects.

The Importance of Gross Profit and Gross Profit Margin

The next things Brent talked about were *gross profit* and *gross profit margin percent*. You get to gross profit after backing out *cost of goods sold*. Gross profit margin percent is calculated by dividing gross profit by revenue. He explained that he looks at gross profit margin percent because it is a more accurate picture of what's going on with a company. A company can be growing revenue and producing higher gross profit in total dollars, but if their cost of goods is going up as a percentage of revenue at a faster rate, it might indicate problems in their manufacturing organization or in sales.

National Products' *Gross Profit*

Gross profit is the first line of defense when running a business. Gross profit and gross profit percent are two of the most-watched metrics of any company. Here again, National Products was in pain, BIG pain!

Fiscal Year	2012	% Change	2011	2010
Revenue	$9.75B	+1%	$9.67B	$9.77B
COGS	$6.71B	+3.4%	$6.49B	$6.45B
Gross Profit	$3.04B	-4.4%	$3.18B	$3.32B
Gross Profit Margin %	31.2%	-1.70%	32.9%	34%

Gross profit is essentially the money a company has left over to fund the rest of the business after they cover COGS. When gross profit is squeezed, it puts tremendous pressure on the business. It is really a snapshot of how well a company is competing in the market. If gross profit is down, you might infer that they are losing profitable customers or discounting to maintain market share, or that they have become unproductive in manufacturing their products.

Gross profit margin percent is a very telling metric. It is calculated by dividing revenue by gross profit. For National Products, after they paid COGS, they had 32.9 cents left over to fund the company in 2011. It dropped to 31.2% in 2012. This meant there was only 31.2 cents of every dollar of revenue to fund the company. This metric is used by Wall Street analysts to look at trends in the business and to determine whether a company is winning against competitors, meeting its economic challenges, and continuously improving its business processes to remain profitable.

In National Products' quarterly earnings call with analysts, one of them asked John Fuller what the company was doing to grow revenue and lower COGS. She expressed concern that these were critical drivers her firm was looking at and was comparing it to those of other leaders in National Products' market. Ouch! We know that the existing trend at National would be bad for the stock if investors believed it was going to continue. If I could translate my solution into profit improvement via improved revenue and lower COGS, I would definitely be able to differentiate my product from my competitors'.

It was clear from looking at revenue, gross profit, and gross profit margin that National Products was trending in the wrong direction. Growing revenue and lowering COGS were bound to be the centerpiece of their financial strategies. Now I felt I knew exactly what had given birth to the quality improvement project.

National Products' *Operating Expenses*

In a stock broker's world, expense management is about how a company operates its business efficiently. To determine that, he looks at their business model. Do they have a large infrastructure supporting their revenue engine? Do they employ large numbers of salespeople, service people, or technical experts? Do they sell through distribution? If so what is happening in that market?

I look at National Products' operating expense (SG&A) line because I know that there are multiple ways I can impact costs through greater effectiveness or efficiencies. For instance, High Beam's new Intelligent Monitor software can reduce the number of hours it takes to gather and report on production. Every dollar we can take out drops straight to operating profit. National's expense management profile looked like this:

Fiscal Year	2012	% Change	2011	2010
Operating Expense	$1.74B	+5.2%	$1.65B	$1.52B
Operating Expense Ratio %	17.9%	+.8%	17.1%	15.6%

Their operating expenses increased more than 5% at a time when their revenues were up only 1%. Their operating expenses as a percentage of revenue were 17.9%. Essentially, it cost 17.1 cents to generate a dollar of revenue in 2011 and 17.9 cents in 2012. That was the trend in the previous year too, so it signified that the company had become less efficient, meaning one of two things. Either they needed to grow revenues at a faster rate with the existing infrastructure, or they needed to cut costs, which usually includes cutting people. There are of course other ways to cut; basically anything discretionary gets the knife.

So there was obviously real pain at National Products, and it was connected to the project. When I asked John Fuller about it, he told me that they were seeking ways to be more efficient, due to the increased maintenance costs, the transportation costs associated with expediting shipments, and the cost of returned product. The last thing he wanted to do was downsize the staff to make up for the higher operational costs.

Operating Efficiency

Operating efficiency is one reason salespeople experience so many challenges in this weak economy. When a company attempts to get lean, every expenditure is under the microscope. Senior management will pressure all departments to cut; squeezing every dollar becomes a fixation. And even when companies do grow during a weak economy, they keep operating expenses in check to ensure that spending doesn't get ahead of revenue, in case there is another shock to the market. They want to make sure they can deliver operating profit at their target levels..

National Products' *Operating Profit*

Operating profit is a measure of how well a CEO is running the business. Operating profit is the profit earned after COGS and all overhead expenses are deducted. It directly affects a company's ability to invest in the business and to deliver shareholder return in the form of earnings per share. Operating profit for National Products was down 15%. That was brutal!

Fiscal Year	2012	% Change	2011	2010
Revenue	$9.75B	+1%	$9.67B	$9.77B
COGS	$6.71B	+3.4%	$6.49B	$6.45B
Gross Profit	$3.04B	-4.4%	$3.18B	$3.32B
Gross Profit Margin %	31.2%	-1.70%	32.9%	34%
Operating Expense	$1.74B	+5.2%	$1.65B	$1.52B
Operating Expense Ratio %	17.9%	+.8%	17.1%	15.6%
Operating Profit	$1.29B	-15.1%	$1.52B	$1.80B
Operating Profit Margin %	13.3%	-2.5%	15.8%	18.4%

I also checked out another important ratio: operating profit margin percent, which is operating profit divided by revenue. It tells you how well a company performed after all expenses were deducted, and it is the most visible number to analysts and shareholders assessing how well the leadership team executed their business plan and strategies. In short, it is a productivity measure. So while National Products made a significant profit, it was substantially lower than in the previous two years. No wonder there was so much pressure on National Products' entire executive team. And no wonder they had made financial rigor and accountability an enterprise-wide effort.

Why Defending Price Is Important to *Your* Business

Being a Profit Hero means delivering profitability to customers through your products and services. But another reason selling profitability is so important is the impact your selling efforts have on *your* company's operating profit. Executives tell me that the number one way to improve profitability of their companies is to defend pricing. Discounts are always going to be part of any business exchange at some level. The question is, *can you defend your margins by selling customers on the financial impact you deliver?*

McKinsey & Company did a study of pricing and found that a 1% price increase will deliver 8% to 10% in operating profit. Conversely, if you discount 1%, it will diminish operating profit by 8% to 10%. A 5% discount would require a company to generate 18.7% greater sales volume to make up for the operating profit given away. *That* is why executive leadership is focused on defending pricing.

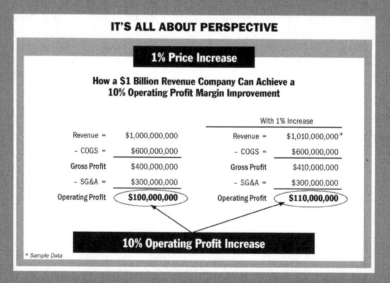

Source: Michael V. Marn, Eric V. Roegner, and Craig C. Zawada, "The Power of Pricing—Transaction Pricing Is the Key to Surviving the Current Downturn—and to Flourishing When Conditions Improve," February 2003,

National Products' *Asset Management*

That was only half of my financial analysis. Now I turned to National Products' balance sheet to see what was going on with the capital side of their business. The balance sheet is revealing, but I try not to get lost in it. You can overanalyze anything.

Current Assets

The key was seeing what was happening in the areas I could impact with my products and services. I knew there was a problem with inventory because of the product that was sitting and waiting to be finished before it could ship. It had been produced but now was just sitting in inventory not doing anything. I also noted that inventories had spiked slightly, which is never a good thing, because inventory ties up cash. And I knew from the company's annual report that National wanted to generate more cash, not less. Accounts receivable (AR) is the other key area of current assets. We couldn't do much to affect receivables, although I have seen that when customers discover defective product, they will slow down payment and also ask for compensation. In the classic scenario, the customer acknowledges receiving your invoice, but informs you it has to be adjusted for returns before they will pay it—and sometimes they wait until it is past due to tell you that. Once you get it corrected, they put it back into the 60- or 90-day queue.

Fixed Assets

I was interested in fixed assets because so much of what High Beam provides affects the manufacturing side of the business. New plants, facility upgrades, and expansion require capital. If fixed assets are flat or trending down, or if their capital expenditures were being cut back, I needed to know. As a result of the Production Quality

Improvement Initiative, National Products was planning on a sizable capital expenditure but it hadn't shown up yet on any of their financial statements. But I did learn later, during my meeting with National Product's CFO John Fuller that it was an investment that was planned and budgeted for the following year.

Return on Assets

Return on assets (ROA) tells you what earnings were generated from invested capital (total assets). ROA for public companies can vary substantially from industry to industry. This is why, when using ROA as a comparative measure, it is best to compare it against a company's previous ROA numbers or the ROA of a similar company. You want to know how the C-suite views their ROA performance. Generally, the higher the ROA the better, but it depends on what the targets are and how consistently the management team is able to deliver on its promises to shareholders and Wall Street. So far, my financial analysis revealed that National Products was in pain and in need of help. But I had more to learn about their business.

My Understanding of What Was Happening in National Product's Business

To understand a company's business, the obvious place to start is with their own explanation of the business they're in. I start with the annual 10-K report found on the company's Investor page. The 10-K is a federally mandated report that all publicly held companies must supply to current and potential investors and analysts. They are all similar in format, but each company determines how much detail to put into the report. It's long— usually about 200 pages of data—but typically 10 pages will give you tremendous insight into the company.

In the first section they describe their business, which gives you an immediate education about *their* language and the terms they use. I can use similar terms later, when I talk to them about their operations, and I'll seem aligned with them. This part of the 10-K tells me what they think is important about their business. They are reporting their performance but at the same time attempting to sell the strength of the company to potential investors.

In looking at National Products' 10-K, I noticed their reporting segments (separate divisions or companies that report separately). Until then, I hadn't realized they had a water filtration unit focused on consumer products and integrated with their fixtures, and also a fast-growing industrial division that was competing heavily in the water purification, filtration, and sustainability space. This was a gold nugget for me because, although the project didn't include those businesses, I now knew that I could show overall profitability and ways we could also have an impact on their business outside of the fixture manufacturing group.

The 10-K goes on to describe how the company is structured, the performance of their reporting segments, and the products and services delivered by each segment. I was intrigued to see that National Products had an emerging—and significant—business in the water filtration market. Since High Beam now has a water filtration division with industry-leading products and technology, I could see my path to leveraging our business across the corporation. National provided the financials for each segment, so I had a sense of the contribution that division was making to the corporation. If I was going to target and approach a division president, I needed to know their profitability by segment.

Customers

Companies often disclose their customers on their websites and in the 10-K, and sometimes even the percentage of business they do with each one. One reason is that investors want to know their exposure. If a company relies too much on a particular set of customers, revenue could be at risk if those relationships sour, if there is competitive encroachment, or if market changes reduce the customers' ability to buy. For me, the customer list is important early on in my discovery process because I want to see if I can identify ways to support a company's revenue growth through their customers.

National Products' 10-K revealed that that three of the big-box retailers were key customers, accounting for more than 10% of National Products' earnings. Since the company was undertaking a quality improvement initiative, I wanted to gauge the impact of poor quality on their revenue and their relationship with these big customers. Another of my customers had once lost the business of a big-box retailer because of poor product quality and shortages. It killed their revenue, and they were three years getting back in the door.

In looking at National Products' customers, I also wanted to see if the buying power of the mass merchandisers was putting greater pressure on National Products' pricing, and if so, how that was affecting profitability—because I thought I could find a quantifiable way to impact that. (I did so ultimately by uncovering the number of incidents where they were shorting customers. I made a strong point about their revenue risks if they didn't get their arms around the problem quickly.)

Competition

The 10-K also features a company's major competitors and competitive issues. National Products named three of their competitors and noted that that the competition kept them under continued product quality, price, delivery, and service challenges. They also pointed out other factors affecting competition, including short-term market share objectives, short-term profit objectives, exchange rate fluctuations, technology, product support, distribution strength, and advertising. They asserted very strongly their belief that technology, product quality, distribution, marketing, and service reputation had given them strong brand name recognition and enhanced their competitive position.

Market Trends / Industry Information

Some companies' 10-Ks include extremely valuable information about their industry, market trends, and forecasts for the future. This is useful when analyzing a customer's business, but also for checking out other companies in the same industry. National Products did not go into depth about their industry, but they did mention the impact government policy was having on their business, including forcing them to adapt to healthcare reform and EPA standards that raise energy costs.

The following box shows how Community Health Systems, Inc., described its own industry's trends in its 10-K for 2012.

COMMUNITY HEALTH SYSTEMS, INC.
Form 10 -K
Year Ending December 31, 2012

ITEM 1. *Business*
Industry Overview

The Centers for Medicare and Medicaid Services, or CMS, reported that in 2011 total U.S. healthcare expenditures grew by 3.9% to approximately $2.7 trillion. CMS also projected total U.S. healthcare spending to grow by 4.2% in 2012 and by an average of 5.7% annually from 2011 through 2021. By these estimates, healthcare expenditures will account for approximately $4.8 trillion, or 19.6% of the total U.S. gross domestic product, by 2021.

Hospital services, the market within the healthcare industry in which we operate, is the largest single category of healthcare at 31.5% of total healthcare spending in 2011, or approximately $850.6 billion, as reported by CMS. CMS projects the hospital services category to grow by at least 4.1% per year through 2021. It expects growth in hospital healthcare spending to continue due to the aging of the U.S. population and consumer demand for expanded medical services. As hospitals remain the primary setting for healthcare delivery, CMS expects hospital services to remain the largest category of healthcare spending.

U.S. Hospital Industry. The U.S. hospital industry is broadly defined to include acute care, rehabilitation, and psychiatric facilities that are either public (government owned and operated), not-for-profit private (religious or secular), or for-profit institutions (investor owned). According to the American Hospital Association, there are approximately 5,000 inpatient hospitals in the U.S. which are not-for- profit owned, investor owned, or state or local government owned. Of these hospitals, approximately 40% are located in non-urban communities. We believe that a majority of these hospitals are owned by not-for-profit or governmental entities. These facilities offer a broad range of healthcare services, including internal medicine, general surgery, cardiology, oncology, orthopedics, OB/GYN, and emergency services. In addition, hospitals also offer other ancillary services, including psychiatric, diagnostic, rehabilitation, home care, and outpatient surgery services.

Risk Factors

Companies are required to outline their risk factors in the 10-K report. They must fully disclose the things that can go wrong in their business that may affect their ability to execute their business plan and deliver profitability. I think a lot of people thumb through this section believing that companies provide little more than perfunctory and already well-known information. Sure, we know that if a nuclear bomb goes off anywhere in the world there could be material impact on the business. But I also sometimes find gems that give me insights into things that I can influence.

If I can quantify how my solution will help a company avoid problems, I can link it to their ability to achieve their profitability goals. If I am able to show a broad grasp of their business, this also provides me just one more way to differentiate my firm from my competitors. Here risk factors mentioned in National Products' 10-K helped me position the ways Intelligent Monitor could support their business and profit goals:

NATIONAL PRODUCTS
Form 10-K

Risk Factors

If the Company is unable to successfully manage its enterprise initiatives, financial results could be adversely impacted.

The Company has begun executing new long-term enterprise initiatives: quality production improvement, strategic sourcing, and ERP implementation. These initiatives include the scaling up of smaller businesses into larger businesses, better leveraging of purchasing power, and leveraging information technology for differentiation and growth potential. If the Company is unable to retain its key employees, successfully integrate ERP, maintain productivity, or otherwise implement these initiatives without material disruption to its businesses, financial results could be adversely impacted.

National Products' Key Strategies and Initiatives

Not every company discloses their key strategies or initiatives publicly, but when they do, you can identify specific profit improvement targets that align with their priorities. When I reviewed National Products' 10-K, I found an initiative called WOW (War on Waste) that was part of an overall sustainability drive that manufacturing and marketing communications were partnering on to get the message out that they were an eco-friendly company. Here again, this was something I could factor into my approach since High Beam has ways of calculating the spray gun excess paint capture with our new spray capture hoods that encompass the work area. I thought I could make a few points just by bringing it up. Besides, sustainability is fast becoming a profit driver for many industries.

I also noticed that they had a Strategic Sourcing Initiative focused on lowering costs across National Products' businesses. They want to leverage their purchasing scale to enhance profitability and global competitiveness. This initiative will transform sourcing into a core strategic function and will build capabilities at both the enterprise and division levels. I knew that their procurement team would continue to focus on price. Let's face it, this is purely a lowest price, supplier reduction plan. I needed to be aware of it so I could navigate it.

After reviewing their 10-K report and other documents, including the industry presentation the CEO made six months ago, I was able to distill National Products' strategies down to the following:

- Generate greater revenue from high-end fixtures through major retailer and commercial supply houses.
- Grow revenue 10% through new revenue streams (core business plus consumer and industrial water filtration businesses)
- Implement a strategic sourcing initiative to drive cost savings
- Reduce costs by improving the quality of the production processes
- Continue to leverage the ERP systems across the corporation
- Generate 4% to 5% free cash flow (cash from operating activities); improve working capital by reducing inventory and speeding up accounts receivables

I knew that there were a number of ways I could quantify the impact High Beam could deliver in support of their key strategies.

Example Strategies & Initiatives from
ILLINOIS TOOL WORKS (ITW)
Form 10 -K
Year Ending December 31, 2012

ITEM 1. *Business*
80/20 Business Process—Strategies & Initiatives

A key element of the Company's business strategy is its continuous 80/20 business process for both existing businesses and new acquisitions. The basic concept of this 80/20 business process is to focus on what is most important (the 20% of the items that account for 80% of the value) and to spend less time and resources on the less important (the 80% of the items that account for 20% of the value).

The Company's operations use this 80/20 business process to simplify and focus on the key parts of their business, and as a result, reduce complexity that often disguises what is truly important. The Company's operations utilize the 80/20 process in various aspects of their business. Common applications of the 80/20 business process include:

- Simplifying product lines by reducing the number of products offered by combining the features of similar products, outsourcing products or, as a last resort, eliminating low-value products
- Segmenting the customer base by focusing on the 80/20 customers separately and finding alternative ways to serve the 20/80 customers
- Simplifying the supplier base by partnering with 80/20 suppliers and reducing the number of 20/80 suppliers
- Designing business processes, systems and measurements around the 80/20 activities

The result of the application of this 80/20 business process is that the Company has over time improved its long-term operating and financial performance. These 80/20 efforts can result in restructuring projects that reduce costs and improve margins. Corporate management works closely with those businesses that have operating results below expectations to help those businesses better apply this 80/20 business process and improve their results.

What's Your Customer's Story?

In the movie **School of Rock**, Joe Black tells his 12-year-old students that he is hung over and asks if they know what that means. They all reply, "Yes, it means you are drunk." He answers, "No, it means I was drunk *yesterday*."

Whatever business result you are experiencing, good or bad, it wasn't caused by the decisions you made today. It was influenced by the strategies, investments and the business decisions you made last month, last year or maybe even five years ago.

When CEOs are asked at a shareholder meeting to explain the performance of their company, as well as projections for the future, they often say *"We are poised for growth!"* They then go on to give an impassioned speech on the virtues of their vision, strategy, and leadership team. It may be a realistic view of the business bolstered by recent success, or it may be a happy spin on a less-than-positive reality. Either way, you need to know how to look at a customer's financials and decode the real story that is playing out. Only then can you know what's going on. ***Because every company has a story.***

> *It might be a success story built on years of effective strategies and informed decisions, great execution, and strong results. Or, it might be a company in decline, or worse, one caught in an endless cycle of mediocrity.*
>
> I have found that there is a varnished view of the business that executives are prepared to communicate to further their cause. But there is also an unvarnished reality to every business too. Looking at the income statement or balance sheet, or seeing their cash flow report, really only tells you about past performance. The question is, can you translate financial information into customer knowledge and insight in a way that provides you visibility into future strategies and priorities for which you can position the profit impact of your company's solutions?
>
> So when you read about the CEO's vision and strategy for the business, keep in mind that the company's trajectory was put in place by decisions already made, strategies already deployed, and actions already taken. That is the *real* story.

The final thing I look at is the Shareholder Letter. I find looking at it last helps me put into full context what I just learned about the company and how the CEO is describing their strategies and priorities for the future. When I read National Products' Shareholder Letter one of the stated goals stood out for me. Harold Roth wrote: *"We will better manage our costs, streamline and improve the quality of our production processes, and create new ways of doing things more effectively and efficiently, while enhancing our execution."* That confirmed my initial assessment: The company would be open to an enterprise system that would support their execution.

A Summary of My National Products Analysis

As my dad told me, *"If you can understand a customer's business and interpret their strategies relative to their revenue, cost management, and capital plans then you will set yourself apart from 90% of all the salespeople out there."* By now I had dug through National Products' 10-K, quarterly earnings reports for the previous two quarters, and executive presentations; and I had combined what I learned there with what I already knew about the production quality improvement project. Now I was confident I could deliver a strong profit improvement case about our products and Intelligent Monitor software. I could show them that our solution would address all of their financial goals.

In a nutshell: All of the key financial metrics were pointing in the wrong direction; revenue was stalled, COGS and operating expenses were up, and cash flow was being squeezed by high inventories. They were losing profitability because of an inefficient manufacturing process. COGS was higher owing to increased use of paint and lower throughput. Their operating expenses were higher because of the manual nature of their production monitoring reporting processes and the maintenance and ongoing repairs to their spray guns systems. They were losing revenue because product awaiting touch-up was delayed in getting to the market. The stagnant economy also contributed, but most of these difficulties were self-inflicted.

I built my profit impact solution around the following business drivers. Here is how I planned to present our case to National Products:

- **Grow Revenue**

  High Beam can enhance National Products' revenue by reducing the number of product defects, and we will speed up product to market with fewer missed shipments. We can also provide a lift to National Products' Water Filtration Division with our

Intelligent Monitoring software, which has wireless capability for industrial water systems.

- **Lower COGS**

  Our spray gun systems will be more efficient, there will be fewer over-applications, less paint will be used.

- **Reduce Operating Expenses**

  We will reduce downtime, leading to more productive use of labor. We will be able to reduce maintenance costs thanks to our Intelligent Monitoring software and the just-in-time alerts that will avert unscheduled shutdowns. We will also lower energy costs, thanks to the efficiency of our guns.

- **ERP Integration**

  We will speed up reporting and provide real-time visibility into the production system via the decision support elements of our Intelligent Monitor software. That will reduce the manual aspects of generating the current reports, which will in turn require less manpower and enable decisions to be made faster, thus speeding up production and making more productive use of resources.

- **Inventory**

  We will free up cash that is now tied up in inventory by moving product and speeding up the production cycle, thus reducing inventory to a minimum. That will make the entire supply chain more efficient.

I was feeling good about how well aligned we were with National Products' financial goals, about our ability to quantify the hard-dollar impact of our solutions. I knew we could defend our claims regarding significant profit improvement for National Products.

How Profit Heroes Do It

Profit Heroes use financial and business analysis to differentiate themselves from competitors by:

- Understanding and interpreting the customer's financial performance
- Identifying and communicating the solutions to key business issues that have an impact on financial performance
- Translating business issues into business strategy for improved profitability
- Speaking the language of the C-suite on how customers keep score and make economic decisions.

Chapter 7

Align

Bringing Thought Leadership and Insight to Customers

*"I've learned that people will forget what you said,
people will forget what you did, but people will never
forget how you made them feel."*

—*Maya Angelou*

Your goal is to get to the C-level, but when you get there, you need to be prepared to conduct a good conversation. You only have a few minutes to gain respect and attention. That's what aligning is all about.

We live in a hyper-informed, data-rich, and technology-fueled environment where getting your message out to the right people at the right time through the right channel is becoming a huge challenge. The noise factor in the market has become a distraction. To get a compelling and meaningful message to a target audience requires a new way of thinking about marketing. And as social networking has become a powerful force in reaching and connecting with customers, it leaves many asking, "Why do I want to talk to you? What benefit will I receive by engaging with you or your company? What are you bringing to the party that is different from your competitors?"

The latest trend in marketing is called "content marketing." At the center of content marketing is a growing emphasis on thought leadership, and for good reason. According to Roper Public Affairs,[3] 80% of business decision makers prefer to get company information from thought-leading articles or white papers, rather than from an advertisement or a brochure. Most executives don't want to be sold to; they want to be informed about trends in their industry, and they want information that supports decisions around strategy, leadership, and capital investments.

More and more industry-leading companies are investing in strong content marketing. Early big players in this space were large consulting companies, such as McKinsey, PriceWaterhouseCoopers, and Accenture, where thought leadership is part of their DNA and is used to create demand for their services. The same is true for technology companies like SAP and IBM in areas such as comprehensive data analytics and application lifecycles. These firms spend a lot of time researching and writing studies that define a new problem, or redefine an existing problem with new implications. They provide industry-specific research, case studies, and white papers that support their areas of expertise and ultimately their solutions. As a result, thought leadership has become a competitive necessity. Companies don't want to be perceived as not having leading-edge ideas in dealing with customers' business challenges.

Content marketing is being used to bring new information in new ways that intrigue, challenge, and even inspire decision makers to engage in a conversation. Strong thought leadership can help start a relationship where none exists, or it can enhance existing relationships. It is about being an authority on relevant business- or industry-specific topics that answer big questions or raise questions that customers have yet to ask. Thought leaders back up their ideas with compelling financial evidence.

---

[3]   Useful content should be at the core of your marketing. See "What is Content Marketing?" http://contentmarketinginstitute.com/what-is-content-marketing/.

The Distinction between Thought Leadership and Insight

Thought leadership is intended to intrigue—to spark a conversation and create an interaction around the questions or issues that matter to the customer. It is about getting attention, creating an awareness of a business or financial issue that executive-level decision makers are concerned about. It can create awareness that provides credibility. It can shape a company's image in a specific space that might be part of an evolving go-to-market sales strategy.

Insight, on the other hand, goes beyond educating and sparking a conversation. It informs decision making. Based on specific customized and validated ideas that have been proven to work, insight is about translating operational and financial information into an actionable plan that can deliver economic impact. High Beam's Susan Stafford provided thought leadership around the latest strategies and technologies for integrating production monitoring systems with an ERP system. She then brought insight when she crafted an approach that could accelerate the operational and financial outcomes that National Products was seeking through its production quality improvement project.

Thought Leadership and Insight Are Important to Selling Profit Improvement

One risk of relying heavily on content marketing and thought leadership to communicate and to engage with decision makers is that, if it works, competitors will copy it. Just as the introduction of a new product or service quickly gets replicated by competitors, so too will your new ideas be co-opted. The task of staying ahead of someone else's research or new ideas will grow more intense in order that it not become commoditized.

There are two ways that thought leadership and insight can remain differentiated. First, with the increased focus on managing costs and improving profitability, nearly all departments within a company are in a continuous search for ideas that can strengthen their business. Take hospitals, which are under tremendous cost pressures. Today the second largest expense after labor is supplies, which can range from relatively inexpensive bandages and syringes to $20,000 medical devices. Many hospitals still use obsolete and manual processes to manage their supplies, putting them at risk of not having the right product at the right time for the patient. If a manual system has no effective way to track inventory, expensive supplies can get lost or stolen.

Approaching a hospital CFO with best practices from another industry, such as manufacturing, can help them manage their supply chain. I have seen medical device manufacturers and other technology companies bring in new ideas for inventory tracking that provide real-time monitoring of all major devices. By adopting new data standards and mobile technologies, hospitals can reduce waste, inventory, and ensure that their billing system is capturing the right information for their reimbursement.

Bringing ideas to healthcare from other industries (such as the auto industry) that have mastered supply chain management can have a significant impact. Thought leadership can be used as a strategy for achieving alignment within or across an organization on a common problem, such as managing the supply chain more effectively in a hospital, where most supply management has been focused on clinical needs. Bringing new information, new ways of defining problems, and creative and successful strategies that solve problems, even if they are from an entirely different industry, can serve to accelerate the decision-making process as it generates focus and clarity. I have found that "branding" a problem or an initiative designed to solve a problem, as Susan did by naming her solution for National Products *Data Fusion—Integrated Production Quality Monitoring System*, is a way to communicate, align, and build consensus.

Second, by providing strong economic proof or a way to quantify the impact of a new idea, approach, or solution, thought leadership gets translated into a highly differentiated marketing weapon. Educating yourself and starting a conversation only gets you so far. Backing up your ideas with economic evidence, customized to the customer's situation, is the next level of thought leadership deployment. This, combined with a well-informed profit improvement strategy, can position you as someone who understands the customer's business and is taking on the role of peer in delivering results. That is powerful positioning, and definitely puts you a cut above competitors who don't know how to do this.

I know from experience that CEOs are constantly searching for an edge—for that one idea, piece of information, or data point that can thrust them ahead of market trends, customer demands, or competitive challenges. While they employ strong knowledge leaders within their organizations, they also know that a company can grow insular over time. That is why, when companies and their salespeople bring them thought leadership and insight and help them use it to create competitive advantages or accelerate their strategies, they are likely to find a warm welcome and ready access.

Examples of Thought Leadership and Insight

Ecolab[5] and Grainger[6] are two companies that have used thought leadership and insight to create competitive differentiation. They have been successful in translating business needs or industry trends into financial impact. The text in the following boxes is excerpted from their websites and other public documents.

Ecolab

Ecolab is a chemical company based in St. Paul, MN, that delivers products and services that promote food safety and clean environments, and optimize water and energy use, which improves operational efficiencies for customers in the food, healthcare, energy, hospitality, and industrial markets. To differentiate itself in the market, Ecolab has made sustainability a centerpiece of its sales and marketing strategy. Sustainability has become a salient issue for companies that are under pressure to comply with market trends and regulatory standards. Ecolab is establishing a market leadership role around sustainability and has included it in the company's innovation processes, environmental impact, and standardization of sustainability metrics. The company is active in industry groups focused on developing greenhouse gas mitigation, climate change adaptation, and water stewardship guidance. And Ecolab is helping customers establish sustainable growth benchmarks. These actions serve to position its thought leadership and the company as experts in the field of sustainability.

To provide customers greater insight into how they can achieve a financial return through sustainability, Ecolab introduced eROI™, or "Ecolab Return on Investment." eROI supports the company's "total impact" approach by credibly documenting resource savings across a comprehensive set of sustainability categories. By linking environmental and social metrics to cost savings, they demonstrate the triple-bottom-line (financial, social, and environmental) benefits of sustainability, and help customers understand and track their own progress toward their internal profitability goals.

See http://www.ecolab.com/sustainability

W.W. Grainger

Grainger is North America's leading broad line supplier of maintenance, repair, and operations products to the industrial and commercial markets. The firm is in a highly fragmented industry with thousands of small and large competitors. Years ago Grainger learned that customers were focusing on cost management and not just acquiring products—they were looking for ways to improve productivity and reduce the costs of operating their facilities. They were experiencing rising labor costs, rising energy costs, safety and workers' compensation issues, and more. And the firm learned that the areas of the customers' business they touched—products and services to support maintenance, repair, and operations (MRO)—were not well understood, and customers thought of Grainger primarily when something went wrong.

Grainger began developing new information and better analytics for the procurement process to help customers better understand the drivers behind their rising MRO costs. Through the use of in-depth analytics and procurement tendency studies, combined with a long and successful history of installing comprehensive procurement processes, Grainger brought new thought leadership to the market. It was able to identify the patterns that led to over 40% of a company's MRO spending being unplanned. The company backed that up with the categories of products purchased, quantities, frequency, and other factors that accounted for a significant and unnecessary rise in operating expense. It was able to document that higher labor costs were due to the time and effort required to search and find products, and that higher administrative costs were caused by a lack of knowledge of a broader need across all facilities. MRO is often considered an operating expense line item on the income statement that is not controllable on a larger scale due to the "just-in-time" or "as-needed" nature of the products purchased.

Grainger's leading-edge data and a unique point of view (*their thought leadership*) allowed the firm to demonstrate the inefficiencies companies were experiencing due to poorly documented MRO procurement processes.

Grainger brought insight to customers by providing the specific financial data that demonstrated how the consolidation of MRO spending would lead to greater efficiencies across facilities, higher productivity, and lower labor costs, directly impacting profitability. In doing so, they were also able to show improved cash flow through better inventory management.

See http://www.donscheibenreif.com/media/chicagobooth/; GraingerGSBRoundtable062509v2.pdf.

Susan Stafford says:
How I Approached Thought Leadership and Insight

The question in my mind was, "How can I introduce new ideas for how National Products could seamlessly integrate our spray gun system Intelligent Monitor software with National Products' ERP system including HR, financial, manufacturing and supply chain systems?" In looking at the trends in the industry, and the strength of the research our marketing group had done, I felt there was a story I could tell. In our white paper "Production Quality Monitoring Technologies—The Next Generation," I noticed some research that I felt would get John Fuller's attention. It was centered on cloud computing and how "big data" were being managed in a new and highly affordable way. I wanted to bring that to John's attention without pitching my solution. I wanted it to be simply a "You need to know this" type of overture.

I also wanted to own this space in a way that would help me communicate across more of the organization that this new technology was leading edge and would impact their areas as well. Besides, I needed a way that to convey High Beam's superiority to the products that I was certain Quality Brands was focusing on. I mean, I had the buy-in from the production, technology, and supply chain teams, which all factored into this project. Knowing that so much is now decided through consensus building, I thought I could help myself by helping John and Rich familiarize themselves and their teams with the concept. So I decided to name the initiative for National Products' product quality improvement project *Data Fusion— Integrating Production Quality Monitoring.* I define it as "the process of integrating multiple data and knowledge sources representing the same real-world object into a consistent, accurate, and useful representation." That drew an image for me—one of a single system—and I thought it would capture the attention of John and Rich.

I was right. The first time I used it in my meeting with them, they latched onto it. When I gave them our white paper "Production Quality Monitoring Technologies—The Next Generation," I wanted to show how High Beam was out ahead of the curve. We were asking questions none of our competitors were asking; and quite frankly, not even National Products was asking them. The paper served to define a problem that allowed me to provide the insight and economic impact our solution would deliver. In that way, High Beam was bringing thought leadership to National Products in a way even their own production team hadn't done. What made it so powerful was that I didn't mention my products once. I used "data fusion" as a concept and began to discuss it in terms most relevant to National Products' challenges.

When I introduced data fusion I believed I could back it up with operational and financial impact that would be important to National Products' final choice of which spray gun systems to purchase and install. By "fusing" their need for scaling the ERP system with the production, supply chain, HR, financial, IT, and customer management systems, I was changing the decision criteria. The technology requirements and qualities of each spray gun system were critical, however. Like so many markets and industries, the true difference between our system and Quality Brands' was slim. A good case could be made for either of us.

So, by broadening the scope and working an economic business case for a total retrofit solution, I provided insights that neither the manufacturing team nor my competitor had. Since I doubted Quality Brands would be taking this approach, I, in effect, created competitive immunity for High Beam. Here is how data fusion changed National Products' final decision criteria:

- <u>Revenue Impact</u>. More efficient spray gun systems, reduction in product refinishing, faster production would speed up revenue with the big-box retailers. Intelligent Monitor software provided real-time supply chain optimization, which also got product to market more quickly, leading to increased revenue.

- <u>Material Costs</u>. Productivity, product quality improvement, and lower paint usage impacted COGS.

- <u>Lower Labor Expenses</u>. By integrating the production system real-time monitoring software with the National Products ERP system, which cost over $50 million, they would reduce labor and provide additional return on John Fuller's ERP investment. Any help providing additional justification in the form of cost savings, efficiencies, and reduced labor was going to be huge.

- <u>Generate Cash Flow</u>. Generating additional cash flow was a stated financial goal. The fact that unfinished product would not be sitting on the floor meant less cash tied up in stalled or stationary inventory.

- <u>Improve Gross Margins and Operating Profit</u>. Analyzing financial and business issues helped put a hard-dollar, defendable profit improvement number on their investment, thereby changing the decision from spray guns to profit improvement.

All of this of course played right into my hands in terms of translating my big idea of data fusion (enterprise-wide spray gun system retrofitting and integratable production management monitoring technology) into hard-dollar profit improvement.

How to Use Thought Leadership

The goal of creating thought leadership is to engage an executive-level conversation and drive results. It requires a consistent and diligent effort. It accumulates over time and builds an expanding base of unique intelligence that can help you differentiate yourself and your company from the competition. It can start with a new idea that changes how decision makers view a business challenge, or it can be a big idea that changes the way they see the world (their world especially).

Small yet simple ideas can address important challenges. Disney World solved the problem of long unwieldy lines for their popular amusement rides by setting up elaborate queuing areas (lines). It helped them manage space during peak times, and it helped manage customer expectations by communicating wait times along the way.

Of course once that became the norm, it wasn't long until someone addressed the boredom of waiting in line. Theme park enthusiast Scott Wegener wrote a book called *Things to Do in Theme Park Queues* and created phone apps filled with activities specifically for amusement park lines, many of which could be played in a confined place with limited resources. Disney gets more people through the park and the wireless companies expand utilization.

A Big Idea: Remote Access

First released in 1998, RealVNC's remote access and control software is today used in more than a billion devices. After winning the UK's premier award for innovation in engineering, CEO and founder Andy Harter explained how it became one of the most successful Cambridge University spin-outs of all time. "The idea was simple, but it promised to revolutionize the telecommunications industry forever. Instead of just calling people on your mobile phone, the device would also become a miniature, wireless computer. Using an innovative touchscreen design, users would be able to buy and download programs via an online store". The "broadband phone," as researchers speculatively dubbed it, would put the power of a PC into the owner's pocket, enabling them to take photos, make films, play games, listen to music, and surf the Web.

This, though, was 1999—and the place was not an Apple research lab, but Cambridge, UK. "We knew that the phones of the future would need to do a lot more than just make calls," Andy Harter, who was responsible for the broadband phone project, remembers. "Around 2000, we demonstrated it at the famous Sun Valley summer camp for industry moguls. The room was packed with technology luminaries and CEOs. I'm pretty certain that Bill Gates and Steve Jobs were there."

Seven or eight years before Apple unveiled the iPhone, not everyone really got the point of this idea. Mobile companies, not to mention their customers, simply weren't ready for the type of phone that was being proposed. Expense was a problem, wireless broadband was not commonplace, and there were some technical obstacles to resolve. "There is a saying in the investment community that *being too early is as good as being wrong*," Harter says. "But the concepts we mapped out have undoubtedly lived on."

Source: Cambridge University
http://www.cam.ac.uk/research/features/
remote-takeover-how-realvnc-conquered-the-world

Here are the steps you can take organizationally or as an individual salesperson to use thought leadership effectively:

1. <u>Don't sell</u>. There is nothing impressive about a white paper that defines a problem and then goes on to solve it with the company's own products or solution. It actually becomes a turnoff, and getting your next piece read will be harder. Think of thought leadership as an opportunity to educate without bias.

2. <u>Focus on one thing, not many</u>. If you are trying to get a big idea across or spur action, it is best to narrow each new idea or piece to one topic. If there are other driving factors, use other venues or papers to tie them together. A sequential and logical approach, presented clearly, helps a decision maker to isolate and focus his attention on the areas you need him to focus on.

3. <u>Give it away</u>. I have seen companies try to use thought leadership as a set-up for bringing in revenue. That is, they attach quantifiable benefit that becomes part of a proposal or a negotiated solution. A firm might, for example, offer a free-of-charge assessment associated with a newly identified problem or opportunity it has brought to the customer's attention. If you provide free services, be careful not to imply a business exchange or commitment. Otherwise, charge for the service and don't dilute the thought leadership. Think of thought leadership as building equity for your brand.

4. <u>Target your audience</u>. The most powerful thought leadership goes straight to the specific needs of a specific audience. In the context of selling profit improvement, any thought leadership "big" idea must be accompanied by the economic factors that the big idea will address uniquely for that company and for that economic decision maker. Making your thought leadership so broad that it "works" for multiple industries or businesses can make it too bland for any of them.

Keep an Open Exchange Going

Getting the idea out is the first step. Translating it into economic impact is the desired outcome. That is, ultimately, what a decision maker will act on. Thought leadership is cumulative. That is, it accumulates with discussion among interested parties in your own organization or your customer companies. It may start as your idea, but keeping a channel of communication open earns a salesperson the opportunity to become a resource for new ideas or valuable intelligence, internally or from third-party experts. Here are a few ways you can keep a channel of idea exchange open to executive-level decision makers:

- Articles that are industry- or business-issue-specific to their company. McKinsey offers free articles that can serve as third-party validation for your concepts. They often include research statistics.
- White papers that are internal or industry-related that shed specific light on an important issue the customer is dealing with.
- Websites that offer topical updates or other valuable information
- YouTube speeches or conference presentations

- Technology analysts such as Gartner, IDC, and Forrester provide the latest trends and thought leadership on subjects like global information security or worldwide IT spending.
- Industry analysts: There are top-ranked analysts for each major industry whose insights are often on the leading edge.
- The Understory RAN (Rainforest Action Network) provides the latest information on climate and energy issues. Becker's Hospital Review provides analysis and the latest legal and legislative changes in the healthcare market.
- Research studies: Industry associations such as the Manufacturers Alliance for Productivity and Innovation (MAPI) is a member organization that conducts research focused on issues relevant to manufacturing.

The goal is to communicate with a customer or prospect without selling. It is to deliver valuable information about an idea that informs their decisions and is not about your products and services. If you stick to informing and refrain from pitching, your target audience will ultimately reward you with an opportunity to do business with the company. Good content aimed at specific financial, business, market, or operational issues will stand a much better chance of getting a customer to read, think, and behave differently—and remember you as the source of his/her enlightenment.

How Profit Heroes Do It

Profit Heroes use thought leadership and insight as a strategy to differentiate themselves from competitors by:

- Gaining access to executive-level decision makers by engaging them in a conversation about business-critical issues
- Changing or influencing the buying criteria by introducing new data and customer-specific financial evidence
- Changing the sales process by elevating decision making
- Aligning influencers, subject matter experts, operations contributors, and validators with their new ideas

---

Chapter 8

Engage

Accessing the C-Suite

"When I get ready to talk to people, I spend two thirds of the time thinking about what they want to hear and one third thinking about what I want to say."
—Abraham Lincoln

There has been an undeniable change in the relationships between salespeople and their prospects. Gaining access to the C-suite or higher-level decision makers became more difficult than ever. A very successful salesperson told me recently, *"In the past I could call, email or get a message into a key contact and get a positive response. Today it seems everyone is too busy, not available, or just not interested. Even when I re-craft my message around key issues to draw the executive's attention, I still get little response. It absolutely wasn't that way even a couple of years ago."*

That has been my experience, too. It wasn't too long ago that I sent a highly targeted and customized email to a CEO outlining how my company could directly impact their revenue growth and improve their operating margins, which my research had revealed as two of his highest priorities. The very next day his assistant called me to set up a conference call. That would be a dream scenario today.

I hear from salespeople constantly that there is something going on that is changing how customers communicate and how identifying and accessing economic decision makers has become a game of "Where's Waldo?"

Certainly one reason for increased resistance at the C-level is the fact that so many salespeople are converging there. And one reason for that is the fact that many companies are not achieving the customer share they desire in their top accounts, and it is becoming financially painful to sell at the operational or procurement level—too much pressure on price and too much delay due to risk aversion of the buyers. If salespeople are selling in a transactional way, or selling on price, achieving profitable revenue is very challenging. Competing on financial impact requires getting to the people who make the economic decisions to help you sell the benefits of doing business with your company. You might need to look internally. Are your marketing messages communicating how you can impact a customer's business? Are your salespeople skilled enough to get to the right levels and communicate their impact? Even if they are, is it enough to win on a sustained basis, especially in slow-growth economy?

Barriers to Entry

The barriers of entry to the C-suite are increasing. Talk to any CEO or CFO (if you can!) and they will tell you that they are deluged with solicitations. It is a full-time job just to field the number of hits they get from "vendors" every day. And yet somehow a few still manage to get through.

Two major changes have contributed to the C-suite blockade: technology and the growing influence of gatekeepers. Email solicitations are growing exponentially as virtually every company has engaged in some level of email marketing. Corporate email systems have many more filters and ways to screen incoming messages. Email *does* have an important role, but using it to lob yourself into the C-suite is not a high-probability tactic.

Voice mail is also under siege. It has always been a way for busy executives or their assistants to screen and delete callers. Many executives have their assistants review their emails and voice

Internal Sponsorship

Internal sponsorship is the most common way to gain access to C-level executives. Of course, gaining the right sponsorship is a challenge. The best sponsors are those that have significant position or political power, because they can usually provide the shortest path to the executive suite. But depending on the level where you currently sell, building a case to elevate your proposal requires more than just technical specifications or operational benefits. Gaining sponsorship today now requires contending with a new corporate financial culture that is risk-averse and cost-driven. That requires educating, collaborating, and partnering with key sponsors to help you secure face-time with key decision makers.

There are risks associated with seeking the sponsorship of someone who is in a position to advance your sales pursuit. First, would that person be willing to take the step or put his or her reputation on the line to recommend your solution? Second, is he capable of understanding and embracing what you are trying to do and able to articulate it well? One challenge of handing off the communication of your business proposition to someone else is that it can change in the telling, and, like the proverbial joke passed down the length of the bar, it gets butchered a little more in each telling. Third, what if your potential sponsor doesn't agree with your approach and instead of gaining a sponsor you create an obstacle? So you need to assess the implications and make well-reasoned judgments about the probability that a sponsor will further your cause.

Educating—A profit-centered salesperson is focused on translating operational solutions into profit impact. At the operational level, managers and even department or functional heads are often not fully knowledgeable about the corporation's big-picture economic drivers. They are typically fixated on costs and living within a defined budget. And because there's so much job insecurity, many contacts are initially unwilling to take unnecessary risk. Educating your contact on the profit impact and translating it into "executive speak" will help them understand that what you're really offering is an opportunity for them to get recognition for offering ideas that directly contribute to the executives' goals for cost management, revenue growth or managing capital. If you do this effectively, you can clear the hurdles to being sponsored upward from lower levels in the financial chain.

Collaborating—Educating is the first step. Once you gain support for your idea, in order to get a referral to a higher-level decision maker or influencer, you need to bring your contacts into the process by collaborating on ways to improve your idea. I find operational level and frontline employees will assist if they think it will make them look good—and if they trust you to help them do so. By pointing out the operational benefits and the profitability to be gained, collaborating with operational level contacts as you develop your profit improvement strategy will make them feel a part of the process. Use and acknowledge their ideas to gain their support, making them feel ownership in your solution. This increases the odds they will refer you upward, whether just one level or several levels.

Partnering—Partnering is usually reserved for the higher-level influencers who have access and credibility with the C-level decision makers. It also requires educating and collaborating, but at this level your contacts have skin in the game. This is the point where you know you have their commitment. You need them to have the passion. When you can relate your proposal to a company's big-picture financial, business, and operational goals, you can partner with high-level influencers who have the confidence to take action. The stronger your business case and your ability to back it up, the greater their conviction and the higher the odds of your getting face-time with the C-level.

After Vince Billings lost the National Products deal and got feedback from National's John Fuller and Rich Bacus, he reflected on the role that sponsorship played in his sales strategy. Here's Vince's perspective in his own words: *"I was in a strong position, I had the influencers on my side and I had their commitment. They were sold. What I didn't do, and I suspect my competitor did do, was spend more time with the CFO. Though I met with him and the EVP of manufacturing, I didn't do a thorough enough job of digging into their motivations around this project. I regret that looking back. I would have had a heads-up about the technology and how pivotal it was to the decision. If I had, the door would have been open to get back and confirm and finalize the specs, which had changed."*

External Referrals—
Building an Executive Referral Network

Being a successful profit-centered salesperson opens up an opportunity to gain exposure to higher-level decision makers who can assist you in building an executive-level referral network. It is hard to do business today through cold calling or soliciting new business without a referral from someone who knows you, your company, and the benefits you deliver. It is especially difficult today because of the heavy emphasis by nearly every sales organization on aiming high.

The most successful Profit Heroes I know have built a strong executive referral network. All referral networks are helpful. Getting to the executive decision makers can accelerate the sales cycle, reduce competition, and expose you to new thought leadership that can help you create new demand for your solutions. High-level executives will respond to professional peers who make recommendations around ideas or solutions that might improve their business. To build and nurture an executive referral network is hard work. But it is one of the top best practices Profit Heroes use in building business through referrals.

There are three levels to an executive referral network. First, there are personal contacts that executives have through their current or previous business experience. These are the strongest referrals. Knowing someone well usually implies a greater level of trust and openness. I had that experience recently when I researched a target prospect where I had no previous contact. I explored their website, Data.com, and LinkedIn. I found the names of several executives to contact, and when I searched first-level connections on LinkedIn I found that a division president was linked to a current CEO of one of my current clients. I noticed that they had worked at the same company for a number of years and I could safely assume they probably knew each other.

I sent the CEO a message to ask if he would make an introduction. He said he knew the president well and would be pleased to help. He then asked that I send him a summary or talking points on what I would want to discuss with his former colleague. I responded with a brief but hard-hitting message about the research I had done on their company, as well as issues related to the integration of one of their newly acquired companies. I included some information about the results we had delivered for similar organizations and for my client the CEO (his former colleague), and said I felt it would be beneficial to meet briefly. My referring CEO sent the email message through LinkedIn and I received a response the next day. I sent my referring CEO an email right away to let him know that the president had responded and suggested I arrange with his assistant to set up a meeting with him as soon as possible.

The second level in a referral network is an executive you know who is acquainted with someone who could benefit from your product, but the association between them might have been a working relationship that ended a number of years ago. Even in these circumstances, I still find benefit in making the connection. Leveraging your contact can still get their attention long enough for you to get your message through.

In another situation, a CEO I know sits on the board of directors of one of my target companies. Clearly the person I know has a working relationship with the target company's CEO and CFO, but in these circumstances executives typically don't want to make a recommendation in order to avoid a conflict of interest (or suggest that the target company's CEO isn't doing his job well and needs help). Occasionally, however, executives allow me to use their name and relationship but prefer that I not make it a direct referral. That still gives me a leg up over competitors who can't do that. I can make the connection and earn some credibility for getting the prospect's attention.

The third level of referral is through peer association. When there is a company you want access to and you have exhausted your contacts and referral resources, contacting executives and referencing industry peers can get their attention. For example, there was a CEO I wanted to reach at a global distributor of communication and security products, but I didn't have contacts who could help me. In my research I saw that the CEO referred numerous times to the leading-edge practices of a prominent industrial distributor (a non-competitor). That distributor happens to be a customer of mine with whom I've had a great deal of success. I was able to identify two or three key success factors that I knew were important to the CEO at the firm I wanted to reach, and by targeting my message to support that firm's strategies I was able to get the executive's attention. In my communication with his assistant I mentioned the interest her CEO had in the other distributor, and our experience, and that I felt he would be interested in some of the ways we could help his business. This approach established relevance and a connection that elevated the salience of my message.

All three approaches can work, but each one requires a specific set of steps that will increase your odds of securing an executive-level referral and a meeting.

Target your request. Your goal is not just to ask for names, but to get help from a referring executive to make an introduction and secure a meeting with a target executive. To find out who executives are connected to, start by exploring tools such as LinkedIn, Hoovers.com, Data.com, and ZoomInfo.com. First-level connections are usually a good bet. Also, look at the companies an executive has worked for previously. The executives they used to work with are rich targets. If they sit on another company's board of directors, they work closely with other high-level decision makers and influencers who can assist you in building a network and securing introductions.

Develop a message. The first thing your executive referral source will want is a brief explanation of why you want to reach a certain person. Your explanation should always include the profit improvement you have helped your customers achieve, but it also needs to zero in on a specific business or financial need or issue. From your discovery analysis, you need to grab onto one or two issues that will pique the interest of the target executive *and* the referral target. Referring to the target company's financial goals or a key financial driver will demonstrate a working knowledge of their business.

If a company has a publicly stated goal to achieve cost reductions of $50 million, embedding your recognition of that goal in your message, along with an example or idea, adds credibility. It also makes it easier for your referring executive to assert urgency and conviction as to why they should meet with you or at least take your call. Susan Stafford of High Beam helped her referral source by articulating in specific terms why it was important to meet (*"I understand that, as part of your need to grow revenue by 10%, improve margins by 2%, and speed up cash flow by $50 million, you are planning to invest in your production facilities to improve quality"*).

Take action. Once you get approval and your executive agrees to serve as a referral, you need to act quickly. You might suggest a phone call or an email. Some very busy executives ask their assistants to send an email on their behalf. All the more reason to have a message crafted that you can pass along. Also, it is important to contact the target executive's assistant and introduce yourself. Assistants have a long list of to-do's, and anything that doesn't get followed up on quickly may not survive.

Report back. Communicating with your referring executive is critical. Provide periodic updates on your progress in securing the meeting, the level of interest the contact expressed and why, and your next steps. A referring executive wants to know that the referral benefited both the customer and you. Remember that their credibility is on the line, and they don't want refer their colleagues to potential vendors or ideas they are not interested or don't see the benefit of exploring. It is up to you to guide the process in a way that makes sure everyone wins. Even if you encounter a lack of action due to timing or circumstance, be sure to communicate in a way that builds trust with your referral source.

Acknowledge. When you achieve success as the result of a referral, it is critical to acknowledge your referring executive. They will want to know that they made a difference by orchestrating an introduction. Your solution could also have the side benefit of being of interest to your referring executive and be a backdoor opening to other opportunities. Your proven success could come full circle, creating a solution for two customers. When I have success and acknowledge my referral source, it is one of my most rewarding experiences in sales.

Direct Contact

The third way to gain access to executive level decision makers is through direct contact, or prospecting. Clearly, establishing direct contact is challenging. You don't have somebody else's name to use in establishing a connection; you are basically a stranger to executives and their assistants, who are already slammed. Here are few things you can do to improve the odds of making your direct contact work.

- Create a message that directly supports a high-priority initiative, a financial goal or "pain" you can identify that relates to their business situation. For the executives at National Products, that included the financial impact of an ERP-integrated solution that would improve production quality. Knowing that National Products had spent $50 million on their ERP system (that sort of news is usually mentioned in a firm's quarterly or annual reports), pointing out one or two strategies that would provide additional ROI lift on their ERP system, as your solution has done for other companies, would likely get CFO John Fuller's attention.

- Lead with financial impact. Executives will respond to a message that directly addresses their financial goals or challenges. I used this approach to secure a meeting with the president of a telecommunications hardware company that was experiencing serious margin problems. It was made very public that they were in an almost desperate situation. I sent him a letter with an overview of a recent client success where we had addressed margin compression in specific and highly relevant ways, and I told him what we did to drive immediate results. I got a call from his assistant two days after I sent my letter.

The best way to answer the question of why an executive should spend time with you is *financial impact*. They pay a lot of people to analyze suppliers' offerings; there are functions and departments that deal with everything and anything a company is pitching. But those who grab attention through the financial implications set themselves apart from the product-centered sellers.

Susan Stafford says:
My Approach to Accessing the C-Suite

After a number of years in sales and working with senior executives, I realized how valuable their insights could be to me in dealing with other executives. I was getting really frustrated with the challenges of reaching the C-suite and decided to ask one of the CFOs I had a strong relationship with how she dealt with all of the solicitations she received every day. First, she said that her longtime assistant did 99% of the screening of all outside calls. Over time she had coached her assistant on what things she would be interested in hearing about, often based on what was happening within the company. For example, with the tremendous uncertainty created by the Affordable Care Act and the impact on company financials, a new firm approached her assistant about an online service that allowed employees to receive medical attention online. It was designed to supplement current insurance while providing significant cost savings. Her assistant understood the urgency of the issue and scheduled a conference call with the CFO. She told me that even though she prefers to deal with people she knows or those who are referred by people she knows, receiving a timely message that addresses a critical business issue is one of the other ways she and her assistant determine whether she should invest her time.

I always start with referrals—executive-level referrals when I can get them. It is extremely hard to cold-call anyone at any level. I use five steps in approaching the C-suite:

- **Focus my search.** I research a company to identify all of the key names and influencers I may want to contact. I always go right to the top, but having a fallback is important. If getting to the CEO isn't possible, I make sure that I have the name and role of a division president or a functional leader who can be a conduit to the CEO or CFO. Those fallback names can come in handy when the CEO's assistant is filtering your inquiry for a place to send you. You can engineer an "internal referral" on the spot by having a specific fallback name and title and asking the CEO's assistant for his or her number and the name of that person's assistant.

- **Research.** I then dig for everything I can find on the top five contacts: current job, previous companies, jobs, and roles. I look for press releases that describe their role in the organization (e.g., "Jim Harris will be heading up manufacturing, supply chain management, and product development"). Tools like LinkedIn are critical for finding connections. That is what I did with National Products. It doesn't always work out that way, but I have been surprised how many connections I can find that I can engineer a referral from. You can also learn a lot about an executive from what they say about themselves in their profiles. Here is what one operations executive wrote about his capabilities and experience in his LinkedIn profile. I found it to be very illuminating and an excellent overview of what he was focused on in his current role: *"Improving the operational performance against a baseline of specific metrics aimed at implementing a supply chain network optimization plan—to improve the cost effectiveness, efficiency, and performance of the distribution network. Specialties include: Key Supply Chain areas of developing and designing distribution networks, transportation strategies and initiatives, and inventory/purchasing management. Also a strong background in financial analysis and managing P/L profitability"*

- **Make a connection or contact**. Using Andy Cooper as a reference really helped me get the meeting with John Fuller. I could not have done it without seeing the connection on LinkedIn. Before asking for help from a referral source, I always frame up why I want to contact an executive—what

I believe is in it for them—and then prepare talking points to make the step of actually contacting and communicating easy for my referral source. Of course, sometimes one of your contacts will ask that you simply refer to your relationship and make the contact yourself. But be bold and ask your referring executive to reach out, and offer to write the talking points. I did that, and Andy jumped on it.

- **Prepare a message.** The hard part is getting enough of the right information so that you can construct a message that gets a specific executive's attention (as well as the assistant's attention). Experience has taught me that using their numbers, drawing out *their* specific financial goals or challenges, is the most important part of the message. Then, it is key to add a very brief but hard-hitting message about how you can impact their profitability.

- **Work with the executive assistant**. I spoke to the CFOs' her assistant about how salespeople approach her. I was surprised to learn how poorly some salespeople do it. Sometimes they are condescending; they badger the assistants or try to go around or over them and sometimes just plain treat them like dirt. They don't seem to understand the clout executive assistants have. In the end, you must bond with executive assistants, acknowledge how busy they are and how important their role is, and attempt to bring them into the process by educating them on why the executive will profit by spending time with you. Be prepared to answer the following questions:

  - What is this about? *(Does it warrant the executive's time?)*

    You need to answer this question with a brief, relevant statement. I want to speak to the executive about a breakthrough approach to leveraging your ERP system, which we have shown can deliver $10 million in improved operating profitability. The CEO mentioned in his last earnings call that that was a priority.

• What does your company do? *(What other functional area can I refer this person to?)*

Careful, this is a trick question. Make it high level and continue to emphasize that what you do is deliver solutions that address the CEO's specific priorities. Otherwise you'll get deferred in the blink of an eye.

• What do you want to discuss with the executive? *(What would the agenda be?)*

Have one or two topics that entice. For example, "I want to share an experience with a similar size company that installed ERP enhanced production software that drove out $10 million in costs the first year."

I always ask for a meeting, usually 30 minutes. That does two things. First, it indicates you will be concise and to the point. It is easier to get on the calendar of a busy executive if you're only asking for 30 minutes. And frankly, if the executive doesn't find the meeting of interest, it is easy to shut it down. My fallback is to ask for a phone call, and that is fine as a fallback, but face-to-face is always better.

Brand Yourself

Branding is usually associated with building market awareness of companies and their products and services. Building a professional brand strategy that communicates your unique knowledge, capabilities, and experiences can help you differentiate yourself from your competition. Social networking has opened up new channels of communication. There are many ways to integrate tools like LinkedIn into your personal branding. On LinkedIn you can link articles and books, areas of interest, and much more to your own profile. You can get help with recommendations that summarize your unique qualities.

Letting your customers know that you are different and that you are a profit-centered business resource helps to establish a perception of who you are and what you bring to the customer relationship. Your brand will set you apart from not only your competitors but also all salespeople selling to a customer. It will differentiate you from your competitors and in fact from any other salesperson who aspires to become a Profit Hero.

- *Develop a tagline.* Write a memorable, meaningful, and concise statement that captures the essence of your personal brand—for example: *Results, No Excuses; Passionate about Customer Success; Profit Seeker.* Put this on your business card or in your email signature.

- *Write an article.* Most salespeople I speak to about this shrink from this challenge, but it's not as hard as it seems. You have a point of view shaped by your unique knowledge and experiences. Not everyone is a writer, but there is assistance within your marketing organization or outside resources that can guide your effort. The marketing organization needs your ideas. I often hear highly experienced salespeople talk about problems they have solved, or new trends they are seeing that can provide very practical ideas, but they don't think of turning those words into a powerful article.

Being published demonstrates to executives and influencers that you are a thought leader in their industry. Submitting articles to associations and other online publications can serve you well. Reaching out to a customer with a targeted thought leadership piece, whether it is a white paper or a personal article, is a great way to engage a conversation.

- *Write a companion message to a white paper.* One of the ways you can personally stand out is to write a highly tailored letter or a short paragraph in an email summarizing a hard-hitting white paper that addresses specific areas of the customer's business or their challenges. By highlighting two or three key learning points you make their reading easier and more engaging. They will remember you for bringing a good piece to their attention. And if they forward it to others, typically your carefully crafted message goes along with it, further spreading your brand.

- *Write a blog.* Contribute a blog on a subject you know, or a trend you see or an experience you or a customer has had that will demonstrate your awareness of industry issues.

- *Leverage your company's thought leadership.* Content marketing is becoming a strong selling tool. Leverage the latest research or industry/customer discoveries that help differentiate you and your company. Be sure to offer your own insight about them. Remember, you are building *your* brand.

- *Be true to your personal brand.* Customers won't return to you or refer you to someone else if you don't deliver on your brand promise.

I have had success writing about subjects I am passionate about. I wrote a white paper titled "Growing Shareholder Value— One Employee at a Time." I sent it out to a number of CEOs and subsequently received an inquiry from a large Fortune 500 company CEO. I also sent it to online sites that I thought might be looking for content; it was picked up by vcapital.com and published online.

Your brand is derived from who you are, who you want to be, and how people perceive you. Your brand is your promise to your customer. It tells them what they can expect from you and how you are differentiated from your competitors. Your brand strategy should include how, what, where, when, and to whom you plan on communicating your message. Becoming a Profit Hero means differentiating yourself around the things that customers care most about: making money. To be viewed as a peer at the executive levels is about selling profit improvement, but it is also about who you are.

How Profit Heroes Do It

Profit Heroes have success accessing the C-Suite by:

- Building and leveraging an executive level referral network
- Utilizing research and the latest business and social networking technologies to target and connect with target executives. Understanding the key financial and business drivers that grab attention and create interest
- Using thought leadership and personal branding to differentiate themselves from competitors as a profit-centered resource when approaching executive level decision makers.
- Securing more C-level meetings than their competitors

Chapter 9

Achieve

Selling Profit Improvement and Proving It!

"You will get all you want in life if you help enough
other people get what they want."

—Zig Ziglar

High Beam Industries won the National Products deal on the strength of their $27 million profit improvement proposal. Susan Stafford and her team understood that what National Products asked for through their RFI and Production Quality Improvement Initiative didn't add up to the best way to achieve their stated financial goals. She knew that the initiative was responding to significant shortcomings in the production system; many technical issues were slowing down throughput, increasing defects and re-finishing rates; and labor expenses were higher because of the aging spray gun systems required so much extra maintenance. And she knew that National Products' software was inadequate in providing real-time executive decision support. To Susan, the way the RFI framed it, the initiative was more about treating symptoms and did not address the long-term financial health of the company.

Selling profit improvement is about doing the right thing, but it is also about doing the right thing in the *right way*. By understanding National Products' business and financial goals Susan made a business case that reflected what executive management needed and wanted by solving their operational needs. But she then took a long-term view in offering a solution that would drive profitability now and well into the future. After meeting with John Fuller and Rich Bacus, Susan knew that she had to build a strategy for helping National Products meet their operational requirements to upgrade the spray gun systems in half of their plants. By seeding the idea of a larger installation, she was now on the hook for making a business case for converting the entire enterprise to a new system.

That was both exciting and scary. She set high expectations and knew that she would need to make the economic case for doing it with High Beam. To do so, she knew she needed a lot more information that would support the specific ways she could impact their key financial drivers. Here is how Susan Stafford developed her profit improvement solution.

Susan Stafford says:
The Profit Analyzer®—Building My Business Case

We have used the High Beam Proposal Generator System for years. It typically builds out the project specifications, installation timelines, and fees. Recently Ralph Morris, EVP of sales, implemented a new tool called the Profit Analyzer, which is designed to help salespeople identify and quantify profit improvement for a customer. It is new, and as an organization we are still working through with customers the best way to utilize it. I felt National Products provided the perfect situation.

The Profit Analyzer allows us to leverage the financial data and pertinent business information from the Business Analyzer (a tool that gives us a company's financials), such as the last three years of financials, key performance ratios, and trends, as well as the business description, reporting segments, strategies, risk factors, and more. That gets loaded into the Profit Analyzer system and allows us to then build a proposal aimed at quantifying profit improvement. Here is the summary page of what we compiled through the Business Analyzer for National Products:

THE BUSINESS ANALYZER — NATIONAL PRODUCTS

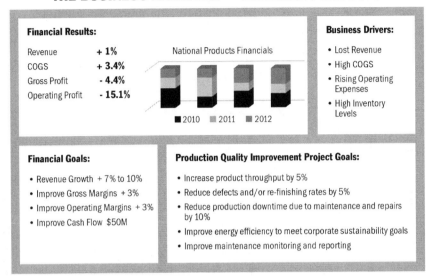

Financial Results:

Revenue	+ 1%
COGS	+ 3.4%
Gross Profit	- 4.4%
Operating Profit	- 15.1%

National Products Financials

■ 2010 ■ 2011 ■ 2012

Business Drivers:

- Lost Revenue
- High COGS
- Rising Operating Expenses
- High Inventory Levels

Financial Goals:

- Revenue Growth + 7% to 10%
- Improve Gross Margins + 3%
- Improve Operating Margins + 3%
- Improve Cash Flow $50M

Production Quality Improvement Project Goals:

- Increase product throughput by 5%
- Reduce defects and/or re-finishing rates by 5%
- Reduce production downtime due to maintenance and repairs by 10%
- Improve energy efficiency to meet corporate sustainability goals
- Improve maintenance monitoring and reporting

The Profit Analyzer is a process and a set of tools that help us quantify and document profit impact. It's very straightforward. Here is the process I used to build my business case for National Products.

Opportunity Analysis
Opportunity: Lost Revenue The business issue: lost revenue to big-box retailers due to product defects, late shipments, and returns
Current Situation
• The goal is to identify the costs impacting business issues *(higher labor, lost revenue, higher COGS, high inventory, high energy cost, lack of efficiency)* • Calculate the total cost of these problems
• The goal is to quantify the impact of solving these problems in hard-dollar terms • The difference between the problems and the solution is the profit impact gained
Profit Impact = $_____

Based on my financial and business analysis of National Products, I had a good plan of attack that included four areas:

1. Capturing lost revenue
2. Lowering cost of goods sold
3. Reducing operating expenses
4. Reducing inventory levels and freeing up cash

From the stated project goals, I knew I needed to show the executives that we were addressing their specific performance metrics, some of which would be included in my profit improvement strategy—for example, increased product throughput, fewer defects, reduced refinishing rates, less downtime, and better maintenance reporting.

Why Profit is So Important

During my presentation to the executives in October, I started out with a slide that was intended to sum up why we were there and what we planned to deliver. By hitting them with a big profit number right at the beginning, I knew I would grab their attention and hold it. Too often, I see salespeople go through a whole litany of slides with information about their company, how long they've been in business, how many locations they have, and on and on. I know executives are not interested in their own company history; all they want to know is, *How will you improve my business? How will you address my business needs and solve my challenges?* And even more than that, top-level decision makers do not want to get into the weeds of a discussion long on technical details and short on proof.

They count on others to know the technical qualifications and requirements. That is one of the reasons I prepared my profit improvement strategy around National Products' financial, business, and operational needs. Because when you think about it, the company's whole Production Quality Improvement Initiative was established because of financial need. Revenue was flat, margins were suffering, and inventory was building up. In the end you have to be able to address all three, but if you start with the economics with a group who lives and dies by the financial health of their business, chances are you are going to align with them quickly.

My Presentation

I branded my presentation and solution *Data Fusion—An Integrated Production Quality Management System.* It was catchy and it had meaning, as I had learned from my earlier meeting with John and Rich. I included the $27 million in profit improvement after backing out the investment. I've found that when you present a solution you can bet that the executives are sitting there thinking, *"This sounds great but what is it going to cost me?"* By putting investment and the operating profit right up front, I quickly got them to focus on ROI. I wanted them to think: *I see the investment and I see the return.* Now you have their attention, and your discussion can turn to how you will help them achieve their return.

The other thing I like to do is to show the impact my profit improvement offer has on their operating profit margin. These guys live for improving operating profit and showing strong upward growth in the percentage, which is an indication that they are managing their company efficiently and effectively. It also goes a long ways in demonstrating that you are a "businessperson." You think like they do, you view the business the way they do. That is, after all, what executive alignment is: living and speaking their language!

High Beam Industries Introduces Data Fusion

An Integrated Production Quality Management System for National Products

Total Profitability

$39,639,100

—$12,215,100 *Investment*

$27,424,000 Operating Profit

Data Fusion will deliver $27,424,000 in Operating Profit or 2.12% increase based on 2012 National Products Operating Profit

$27,424,000 in Operating Profit

Next I pointed out that our plan would add another $10 million over the following two years and that it would require 18 months to install all of the system upgrades and updates. In the end, National

Products would be on the same footing with some the world's most advanced manufacturing companies who are driving production efficiencies, supply chain optimization, and product quality improvement through their ERP and technology organizations.

Quantifying the Opportunities

The next step is to break down how we got to the $27 million number. In building my business case, I made a list of the things I needed to know to support my proposed profit improvement. If I could get information about the causes of their quality problems, and consequently their financial problems, I could quantify the profitability High Beam could deliver. I sent Rich Bacus an email and copied his assistant, noting that I needed a few pieces of information to prepare the proposal options that he and John had requested during our meeting. He shot back a message suggesting I meet with someone on Chet Gretzky's staff to get what I needed. I called Chet, who was helpful but not overly enthusiastic. I still had the feeling that he was heavily in the Quality Products camp and not willing to go out of his way to help me. Nonetheless, I did get the information I needed.

I also emailed John Fuller asking for the name of someone in the IT group who was responsible for the ERP system and the current quality and maintenance reports. He referred me, and I was able to get all of the technical details (IT platforms, software, databases, servers, etc.). With this information I was in a position to build my business case. Here is how it broke out.

Capturing Lost Revenue

I found out that as a result of missed shipments to the big-box retailers, National Products was losing as much as $60 million in revenue from late shipments, defective product and returns that had to be reimbursed. There are costs to that as well. I kept it conservative and though that around $51 million would be the number we could defend by eliminating these production problems.

There was little question that our spray gun systems and especially our Intelligent Monitor software would eliminate all of National Products' lost revenue attributable to poor quality. It would be a 100% certainty *if* they did an enterprise retrofit. Our more efficient spray gun systems would reduce product refinishing. The result would be faster production, which would speed up revenue and prevent lost revenue from the big-box retailers. Intelligent Monitor software provided real-time supply chain optimization, which also got product to market more quickly, leading to increased revenue. The way the numbers broke down was that National Products would recapture or avoid lost revenue at $51 million annually. I used their 13.3% operating margin to calculate profit improvement of over $6.8 million. Here's how I presented it:

Opportunity Analysis: Capturing Lost Revenue

Over $51M in lost revenue to big-box retailers and other segments due to product defects, late shipments, and product returns in National Products' high-end fixtures.

Current Situation
- Average of 3 returns per retail store
- –3 x 12 months = 36 returns annually
- 36 returns x 3,000 stores = 108,000 returns
- **108,000 x $475 revenue per fixture = $51,300,000**

High Beam Solution
- **Revenue recapture 100% through Intelligent Monitor real-time production quality alerts; defective products will not be shipped.**
- **Revenue capture = $51,300,000**
- **$51,300,000 x 13.3% operating profit**

$6,822,900 in Operating Profit

Lowering COGS

I broke down the impact on cost of goods sold into two areas: (1) excess paint usage and (2) added direct labor costs (labor costs associated with the actual production of a product versus operating expenses that support the organization). I made a big point about the application over-spray. With the application of paint at higher densities, especially on their high-end fixtures, high expenditure on paint were having a significant impact on National Products' cost of goods sold and gross margin. It was a direct contributor to their drop in Gross Profit Margin, it showed that they were not managing their production organization as productively as they should have (and their competitors probably were).

We estimated the profitability gained through lower COGS through eliminating excess paint at $13 million. I also included lost direct labor hours, which would generate $7.4 million in improved operating profit. Of course, every dollar of cost reduction we were able to show National Products drops directly to operating profit. I find that salespeople too often compete on cost savings as if that were the end game. For executives, the end game is operating profit and delivering earnings per share.

In other words, if lower COGS or operating expenses directly affects operating profit, why not speak in the language of executives? *You are not just reducing costs; you are improving profitability.* That may seem like a small semantic difference, but to executives who think like that, it actually demonstrates a working knowledge of financial relationships between different aspects of their business. That is how they view the world. You say cost savings, they hear earnings. If every competitor walks in and slams down $1 million in cost savings, the win goes to the "businessperson" who has the big-picture view of the economic decision makers. Here is how I broke out COGS:

Opportunity Analysis—Lowering Cost of Goods Sold—Excess Paint

Due to outdated spray gun systems and poor production quality monitoring, excess paint is being applied to high-end fixtures, unnecessarily raising the cost of goods.

Current Situation

12 gallons of excess paint per day per plant
- 12 gallons x 5 days = 60 gallons per week
- **60 x 4 weeks = 240 gallons per month**
- **240 x 12 months = 2,880 gallons per year**
- **2,880 x 42 plants = 120,900** gallons
- **120,900 x $150 per gallon = $18,135,000**

High Beam Solution

Intelligent Monitoring & new spray gun systems will reduce paint needs by 75% during production.
- **12 gallons x 75% = 9 gallons saved per day per plant**
- **9 gallons x 5 days = 45 gallons per week**
- **45 x 4 weeks = 180 gallons per month**
- **180 x 12 months = 2,160 gallons per year**
- **2,160 x 42 plants = 90,720** gallons
- **90,720 x $150 per gallon = $13,608,000**

$13,608,000 in Operating Profit

Opportunity Analysis: Lowering Cost of Goods Sold—Labor Costs

Additional labor required to change/clear equipment due to outdated spray gun systems and poor production quality monitoring data with excess paint applied to high-end fixtures.

Current Situation
Average 3,200 labor hours per year, per plant
- **3,200 x $85 per hour*= $272,000 per year**
- **$272,000 x 42 plants = $11,424,000**

$11,424,000 extra direct labor costs
* benefits included

High Beam Solution
Intelligent Monitoring & new spray gun systems will reduce labor hours by 65%
- **3,200 x 65% = 2,080 hours saved**
- **2,080 x $85 per hour* = $176,800 per year**
- **$176,800 x 42 plants = $7,425,600**

$7,425,600 in Operating Profit

Reducing Operating Expenses

By integrating the production system real-time monitoring software with its ERP system, which cost over $50 million, National Products would reduce labor and provide additional return on John Fuller's ERP investment. If I could help provide additional justification in the form of cost savings, efficiencies, and reduced labor, it would be huge.

Operating expenses provides a rich opportunity to help any company. It is where most of the company's operating overhead resides: HR, sales, marketing, IT, legal, and more. Production environments are always looking for ways to reduce labor. I often hear from mid-level managers that eliminating labor (jobs) sometimes sends a negative message, although the C-suite knows it is a part of corporate life. No one wants to hire people only to lay them off because of the company's poor performance. But because companies have gotten so lean following the recession, there isn't a lot of room to cut. So when you can show savings that could result in cutting staff, there are a couple of things to remember. First, staff can often be placed in other roles. For instance, IT employees working on an inefficient production reporting system that is replaced with new software can usually be redeployed to another under-staffed project in IT.

Second, if you can make a company more efficient, you slow down the rate at which they have to bring people on. That resonates with the C-level because hiring is an expensive venture that needs to be done in a balanced way. In short, greater efficiency helps them manage their costs going forward. That is one of the reasons you see more and more outsourcing taking place, to reduce the total number of full-time employees.

In my discussions with Rob Hernandez, the National Products plant manager in Texas, I was able to get the efficiency-related answers I needed to formulate my financial impact argument: the number and frequency of assembly line shutdowns due to maintenance and/or equipment repair occurrences; the number of hours engineering spends on repairing equipment, especially during prime production time. With a maintenance and monitoring system, faults can be anticipated and the maintenance and repairs can be made offline, in off hours, thus avoiding the lost labor when employees have to be idle for hours.

Based on the answers I received to my questions, I estimated we could reduce operating expenses in two areas. First, our Intelligent Monitor software would reduce maintenance and repair incidents because of the real-time and wireless alerts that get resources aligned with production needs as they are happening. Second, we could change the labor-intensive way National Products was managing the production and maintenance reporting system they had in place. That was a big win: All together it was worth $9.7 million in improved operating profit.

Opportunity Analysis:
Reducing Operating Expenses

Operating expenses are rising due to increased maintenance and repair incidents resulting from outdated spray gun systems. Also, because of the weak production quality and maintenance reporting system, added labor costs are incurred through the technology group.

Current Situation
2,750 hours for maintenance per plant
- 2,750 x $120* per hour = $330,000
- $330,000 x 42 plants = $13,860,000 582 hours for data / reporting
- 582 hours x $120* per hour = $69,840
- $69,840 x 42 plants = $2,933,280

* benefits included
= $16,793,280

High Beam Solution
Intelligent Monitoring & new spray gun systems will reduce maintenance labor by 60% & IT labor by 50%.
2,750 x 60% = 1,650 hours per plant
- 1,650 x $120* per hour = $198,0000
- $198,000 x 42 plants = $8,316,000
582 x 50% = 291 hours for data / reporting
- 291 hours x $120* per hour = $34,920
- $34,920 x 42 plants = $1,466,640

$8,316,000 = $1,466,640 = $9,782,640

$9,782,640 in Operating Profit

Reducing Inventory Levels

The last area I went after was inventory, which was all connected to the impact of more efficient production, speed, and quality. I showed how inventory building up across all plants was increasing and that when product is pulled off for repaint or touch-up, it ties up capital and increases costs. I showed them that they were actually at greater risk with the big-box retailers as product delivery became an issue, not to mention the lost revenue. Generating cash flow was a stated financial goal. They talked about increasing cash by $50 million. Our Intelligent Monitor software would result in a reduction of at least $20 million in inventory sitting on the floor basically doing nothing. That meant less cash tied up in stalled or stationary inventory. Using a cost of capital of 10% (basically the value of money), we could save National Products the $2 million they were spending to carry unnecessary inventory.

Opportunity Analysis: Reduce Inventory

National Products is experiencing high inventory levels due to substandard quality and backlog for refinishing as a result of poor production quality and monitoring information.

Current Situation
Average inventory on hand = $39,683 per plant
- **$39,683 x 12 months = $476,196**
- **$476,196 x 42 plants = $20,000,232**

$20,000,000 extra inventory being carried

High Beam Solution
Intelligent Monitoring & new spray gun systems will reduce inventory to zero
- **$20,000,000 extra inventory x 10% cost-of-capital* = $2,000,000**

* *The cost of funds used for financing a business*

$2,000,000 in Operating Profit

The iPad Demo

It was time to tie it all together using our iPad demo to show the Intelligent Monitor software set-up for their 42 plants and spray gun systems. During the meeting I handed out iPads to the National Products executives; I told them we would demonstrate the impact of our full retrofit approach using High Beam's Intelligent Monitor software, which brings all of the conversion and enterprise-wide production data to a single desktop. We used a smart phone to demonstrate the wireless feature that notifies the system that quantity of paint, paint application calibration faults are triggered or there is a system shutdown. Again, all of this would be fully integrated with their ERP system. We included an inventory management report and other logistics data to show how the system supports the entire supply chain management process. We gave them a clear working view (albeit only a demo mock-up) of how the system would work. It was a winner, no doubt about it.

Intelligent Monitor iPad Application

I had our CTO Ben Karan cover all of the technical details of our spray gun systems, all the upgrades and enhancements we have made, and how the installation would roll out.

I knew that our proposal was bold and forward-thinking, and I also knew it was supported by hard-dollar numbers that we could defend. Going into an executive presentation knowing that you can deliver over $27 million in improved profitability is a great feeling. Typically, executive presentations can be high-stress situations. But when you're able to put yourself in their shoes and look at the business the way they do, your confidence level skyrockets. Plus, knowing their financial pain, we were able to align with their business needs, which set us apart from Quality Brands, so I was aware of my advantage over my single competitor.

The last slide I showed was a summary of the profitability and the impact on National Products' operating profit, which included:

- Capturing lost revenue = $6,822,900
- Lowering cost of goods sold – excess paint = $13,608,000
- Lowering cost of goods sold – Labor = $7,425,600
- Reduce operating expenses = $9,782,640
- Reduce inventory / cost of capital = $2,000,000
  Total = $27,532,000

The bottom line told the story of how High Beam intended to be an earnings contributor to National Products. It told the assembled executives that choosing us was a sound business *and financial* decision.

The final slide I brought up was intended to show our commitment to ensuring we would stand by our promise of the operating profit we promised. Both Harold and John seemed to really get into it. I could tell that they were taking detailed notes, and as they looked at each other, they seemed to be communicating mutual agreement and delight. Of course, I wanted to think that it was because they were pretty sold on the whole idea. But I am certain in the back of their minds they wanted this commitment to help them to communicate to the board why they were making such a large investment, especially since they had originally forecast a $5 million expenditure.

Our process is flexible based on each organization's structure and constraints. But we got the point across to them that we would stand behind our promises. We had a Profitability Scorecard and process that would make everyone accountable, which executives always love. I didn't go into detail but gave enough information for them to get the picture: We clearly knew what we were talking about and had done it before. I really do think it was the final thing that got us the deal.

Let's Prove It!
Data Fusion Profitability Scorecard: The Process for Tracking & Measuring Results
• Executive Commitment • **Select Project Manager** • **Project Team Assignments** • **Project Team Meeting** • **Establish Project Metrics** • **Identify Existing Reporting System (ERP)** • **Launch Project** • **Schedule Fusion Team Meetings / Executive Briefing** **Meetings** • **One-Year Anniversary—Executive Project Report** • **Executive Communication Employees & the Board**

National Products' Executive Feedback

The reaction of the executive team was strong during the meeting. They told me later that they had been impressed by the approach we took. They had been expecting a technical presentation that focused on the retrofit solution, the installation, and the project costs. Instead, they got a business presentation that focused on their need to drive financial results through an enterprise-wide conversion that totally changed the way they thought about their business and this project. John Fuller said that we redefined how they should be managing production quality and leveraging the latest technology to ensure that they were on the leading edge of production management.

That is what National Products' executive team had aspired to do but had not made that clear in their RFI and the subsequent information they provided. They said that the fact that our solution centered on the Intelligent Monitor software integrated with their

ERP system made the enterprise-wide spray gun system conversion easy to understand. They added that it would help them explain the decision to the board of directors next month. Overall, I felt like I was part of the executive committee. Our conversations and the demeanor of the group were such that I actually felt like a peer working through important business decisions that directly impacted the company's financial performance and ultimately shareholder return.

Prove It!

As Susan demonstrated, regardless of what level of selling you do, you need to batten down the hatches when it comes to proof. Throughout this book I have emphasized the need to understand a customer's business, their financial drivers, and how you can make the case for profit improvement. Decision-makers are determined to hold suppliers accountable for the results they promise. Saying it's so just doesn't convince them any longer.

The most important step in the profit-centered sales process is proving that the profit impact you have proposed will indeed be achieved. That usually brings on a serious case of acid reflux and cold sweats for most salespeople. They know that customers are emphasizing results more than ever before. Offering anecdotal evidence has been an easy way to do deals, especially when you aren't called on it. But "Trust me" doesn't cut it anymore, and neither does throwing out examples of hard-dollar results you've provided to other customers. Executives will tell you, "This is *my* risk. Make me confident about *my* return."

Obstacles

Quantifying financial impact is very challenging. Proving it is even harder. There are four obstacles that Profit Heroes understand when they are called on to prove profit impact:

1. We aren't in control of all of the variables that will impact our solution.
2. We don't have access to the information we need to validate results.
3. We don't have executive or organization-wide support to track, measure, or report on progress; too many things fall through the cracks.
4. There will be external factors, such as the economy and other non-controllable events, that affect the desired outcomes.

There are no easy ways to get around these obstacles, but it is important to mitigate your risks by getting the information and support you need to document profit impact. A profit-centered salesperson knows that proving profit impact is the key to building additional business and to establishing an executive-level referral network. Proven profit impact becomes the relationship currency that ensures continued access to executive decision makers. It is the ticket into the game for becoming a peer when business issues or opportunities surface that you and your organization want to compete for.

The biggest reason most salespeople have difficulty tracking and measuring results is that they don't have the level of executive commitment and engagement required to ensure that all of the other levels involved in deploying the solution know their role, what is expected of them, and that they are being held accountable to support the effort. Basically, you can sell a deal at the operational levels, but directly or indirectly getting support to measure results is the difference between selling a solution and selling profit achievement. It will always require leadership engagement. Here is how Susan Stafford does it.

Susan Stafford says:
My Process for Proving It

I believe proving the profit impact you have on a customer's business actually starts before the sale. We have learned the hard way at High Beam Industries that if we don't establish a well-defined installation strategy, our chances of getting the hard-dollar evidence of our financial impact is diminished dramatically. The way I look at is this: if a customer wants to hold me accountable for results, then I feel like I have the right to hold them accountable to assist me in making it happen.

It is easy to leave the presentation, shake hands, and get the contract process going. Once installation begins, the job becomes all about what was sold, what was bought, and when it will be installed. The process of tracking results is assumed but not operationalized. That's because there is no clearly defined owner of the results. There may be an owner of the installation, but ownership for results often gets missed. So with management's help, I put together a process that I sell during the presentation and then make a part of the customer's deliverables. It is more than a box checked; it becomes integrated into the enterprise-wide installation strategy. Here is the process I use:

Prove It!

Fusion Project Installation & Measurement Profitability Scorecard

Activity

Executive Commitment
- Funding for resources to manage, track results
- Assign project manager
- Communication strategy to organization *(to ensure alignment)*

Select Project Manager
- Job description (High Beam provides)
- Authority levels (High Beam recommendations)
- Role & responsibilities *(High Beam provides)*

Project Team Assignments
- Functional/departmental leads *(production, IT, finance, HR, supply chain, procurement, others)*

Project Team Meeting
- Functional/ departmental leads *(frequency, communication approach)*

Establish Project Metrics
- Operational and financial metrics *(tied to profit improvement solution)*

Identify Existing Reporting System (ERP)
- Identify reporting gaps/requirements
- Build Fusion-specific reports

Launch Project
- Executive kick-off (CEO, CFO)—*(High Beam to provide scripts/talking points)*

Schedule Fusion Team Meetings
- Monthly—provide an agenda *(High Beam to provide)*

Schedule Executive Briefing Meeting
- Monthly—provide an agenda *(High Beam to provide)*

> ### Schedule Fusion Team Meetings
> - Monthly—provide an agenda *(High Beam to provide)*
> ### Schedule Executive Briefing Meeting
> - Monthly—provide an agenda *(High Beam to provide)*
> ### One-Year Anniversary—Executive Project Report
> - Financial Scorecard / Operational Performance
> - Controllable and non-controllable variables
> - Attribution assignments based on financial,
> Operational, and controllable factors
> ### Executive Communication
> - Prepare communication on success for employees and the board of directors
> - Talking points for earnings calls and financial Reporting

I have found that CEOs and CFOs who make a large investment are extremely receptive when they see, early on, a constructive and well-documented approach for measuring results. If you get their commitment right away, chances are much better that you will get the support you need. That was the case with National Products. Harold Roth and John Fuller jumped all over the idea of a Profitability Scorecard and were eager to know what their responsibilities would be and what they could do to support our efforts. They actually had more skin in the game than we did, because it wasn't a performance contract and we were going to get paid either way. But the credibility we earn when we lay out a strong plan engenders a great deal of confidence.

The Profitability Scorecard helps us gain control of all of the variables that will impact our solution. With executive oversight, we will have access to the information we need to validate results. The beauty is that every level knows that whatever their assignment, top management owns it and is heavily invested in success. We still can't prevent external unforeseen events, but by having a thorough reporting process, we can defend the results we get, and we can use that information to draw out the things that are attributable to our solution. It is the best way to get the results you need.

How Profit Heroes Do It

Profit Heroes are committed to selling and proving the impact they deliver by:

- Identifying the business issues that impact their customer's financial performance
- Quantifying the business issues and offering hard- dollar profit improvement strategies that address a customer's financial goals
- Providing a return on investment for their solution
- Ensuring they secure executive commitment to invest in tracking, measuring, reporting, and proving profit improvement

---

Chapter 10

Installing the Profit-Centered Sales Process

"High expectations are the key to everything."
—Sam Walton

How can you do what Susan Stafford did? What does it take to install a profit-centered sales process, and how is it done?

High Beam Industries had begun to invest in tools and resources to assist their sales team in selling to the C-suite. They knew that competing on price was a zero-sum game and that they needed to elevate their message and approach. While it hadn't been fully operationalized, Susan Stafford applied a lot of the new things the company had provided in the way of the Business Analyzer and Profit Analyzer. And she also sought out cross-functional ideas from marketing, product management, IT, and finance to help sell profit improvement as part of her offering to National Products. She led the way and achieved success with a lot of help.

From the autopsy of the National Products success, Julie Moore, High Beam's CEO, determined that they needed to institutionalize the profit-centered sales process that Susan used as their go-to-market sales strategy. Fortunately, Susan had a strong leadership team willing to take risks and to invest in a new and better way of achieving sales success with customers, and against their key competitors.

After finalizing the plans for the Profit Hero of the Year Award, the executive team assigned a top resource from the Organization Development group to work with Susan and sales leaders to develop a strategy for implementing the process, skills, and tools to operationalize the profit-centered selling approach. They put together an installation approach that senior management signed off on and began to formalize the process.

High Beam Industries Installation of The Profit-Centered Sales Process				
Executive Sponsorship	**Organizational Alignment**	**Communication**	**Execution & Accountability**	**Measurement**
• Commitment • Investment & Resources • Program evangelist • Financial goals • Executive engagement	• Management engagement • Roles & responsibilities • Cross- functional work teams • Integrated messaging	• Rollout • Set expectations • Executive overviews • Team communication • Company communication	• Implement training • Deploy Business Analyzer • Deploy Profit Analyzer • Set performance goals • Coaching	• Track results • Data-base profit success stories • Measure customer impact • Measure High Beam Impact

Executive Sponsorship

Commitment

If you're part of the executive leadership, changing how you go to market is a big deal. It involves more than salespeople selling differently. Too often changes are installed, but when executives make decisions or communicate something that conflicts with the new strategy, doubt grows and ultimately there will be resistance to the change. At High Beam, they knew that Julie Moore would need to be a strong voice for the change and to show her commitment to the process.

One of her first strategies was to institute the Profit Hero of the Year Award. That let everyone know that this change in how High Beam was going to market was being driven from the top. But it goes beyond the CEO; all of the executive committee needs to understand and embrace their roles in making it happen. Marketing has to be on board because if the marketing literature or communications goes out with a product-centric message, it will conflict with the strategy of focusing on customer business needs and profitability. The CTO needs to know that there will be new demands for information and data that to support cost and impact calculations in order to demonstrate profit improvement for the customer. Most of all, the entire leadership team needs to know that this is not a temporary change. They need to understand that this type of change will take time and resources to accomplish.

Investment and Dedicated Resources

Many initiatives die before they start because of underfunding. I have seen a lot of organizations that know the right thing to do and say the right things. But they don't back it up with the investment it takes to achieve the desired outcome. There are a couple of reasons for that. First, changing the sales process is tricky; you don't want to disrupt the revenue engine, yet you want the revenue engine to perform at a higher level. I often see a stepped approach, a sort of "earn the funding as you go" approach, but the moment the numbers dip, commitment to the process becomes timid and probably gets shelved "for a short time."

There is no stronger way of showing commitment than making the investment to see the change process through to its completion. That is easy to say, but given the financial pressure on executives today, sometimes not all that easy to do. At High Beam, they had the benefit of seeing the profit-centered sales process play out and deliver big margins to the company. Frankly, the investment needed to deploy the process was easily earned in that one deal.

Typically, a firm needs to invest in new software, training, new tools that help identify and reach the right levels in the prospect firms, marketing support, and IT support. The strategy needs to be fully deployed before all of the results have been banked. That's not an easy decision. Only those with vision do it.

Program Evangelist

Think of the shift to profit-centered selling as a huge campaign. It takes an evangelist to get the word out, to be the constant for the organization when things go sideways or when success becomes elusive. Deals are on the cusp and then lost; once that happens a few times, everyone from the CEO on down to the frontline salesperson starts to question the wisdom of the strategy. That's why there needs to be not just a project manager but a Program Evangelist, someone who will be there 24/7 believing in the cause, espousing the benefits, and picking up those who skin their knees.

High Beam had just the person in Hank Barry. He was a "jack of all trades" manager who was one of the most enthusiastic and positive guys in the company. He was a big believer in the company, its products, and people and had customer-facing experience as well as marketing and manufacturing experience. He was given the title and a raise. He had a big task but was all over it.

Installing a profit-centered selling approach requires someone who is aware of and connected to all of the organizational functions and departments that are needed to support the process. Hank had that reputation, which was key to making it work. He was a liaison who could collaborate, orchestrate resources, and resolve bottlenecks.

Establishing Financial Goals

A company that makes the switch to profit-centered selling needs to establish its own financial goals. Number one is to drive revenue—not incremental revenue but breakthrough revenue. It is like any other investment: If you are going to spend the time and resources, you want to know what the return will be. When it comes to selling profit improvement, it will drive greater revenue per customer (like the National Products deal); instead of waiting in line for procurement to feed you, you are going to the funding source that will help accelerate your growth.

Here were the goals High Beam established in switching to profit-centered selling:

- Raise revenue (from 10% wallet share to an opportunity for $5 million to ultimately $12 million)
- Improve pricing (get a higher average margin on a larger deal)
- Shorten the sales cycle (Susan went from out-of-the-picture to closing the deal in 60 days)
- Win new customers (National Products was essentially a new customer)
- Get paid for services (a higher margin provides cover for extra resources dedicated to the account)

Winning more deals like National Products can transform an organization's financial performance.

Executive Engagement

One of the ways to engage the executive team in the new go-to-market sales strategy is to involve them in it. Julie Moore knew that. That is why she had Susan Stafford, the first official winner of the Profit Hero of the Year Award, spend a day with the executive committee. She had two agendas. First, she wanted to reward Susan and send a message to the entire sales organization that when you achieve that kind of success, you will be recognized. You will have access to the top of your own organization as a "peer." Her second reason was to expose the executives to a salesperson who was reinventing how High Beam did business. After all, they all benefit from this kind of sales success. It gave them a kind of inside-out look at sales. Julie felt they needed to be better connected to the field and to their top salesperson.

It is very refreshing to see the executive committee interact with the sales team more often than at the annual holiday party. They need to understand the kind of people who are carrying the torch for the future of the company.

Organizational Alignment

Management Engagement

Julie knew that changing the culture starts at the top, but she also knew that every level of management must be on board and share the vision. She began the process of getting every manager in the company to understand their sales process by having them look at their own business. As part of her management meetings and her executives' managers' meetings, she began to assert the importance of financial management, paying attention not only to cost management but also to improved profitability. In a sense, she helped managers understand that their jobs are to manage the budget and make good decisions but also to look for ways that their teams or even suppliers can have a greater impact on their business goals. In her own way, she was softening them up for what was just around the corner, with ever-increasing emphasis on customer and company profitably.

Roles and Responsibilities—Cross-Functional Work Teams

Profit-centered selling requires a well-oiled, interactive organization, not a lot of people in siloes who don't talk to one another. For a salesperson to sell profit improvement they need to know how products and services influence the customers' different financial metrics. If you can impact cost of goods sold because your systems reduce excess paint, you can't leave it up to the salesperson to figure that out. Product managers know a lot about the market. They know why customers buy and what their products do to affect the performance of a customer's production system. What is changing is how a salesperson calculates the financial impact and how it can change the game. That is why roles and responsibilities across the organization will need to change. High Beam's Intelligent Monitor software performed some valuable functions, but it wasn't until Susan and the team put it into the context of the entire production system that they were able to capture its unrecognized, greater potential for cost savings and profit impact for the customer.

Integrated Messaging

One big and highly visible indicator of a profit-driven organization is its messaging. Everything from marketing literature, white papers, and brochures to proposals plays a role in conveying the concept of profit impact. One of the biggest gaps in messaging that I see is between sales and marketing/product management. Marketing and product management are by definition product-centric. After all, products are what the company is in the business of producing and selling. However, when a company makes the shift to profit improvement, the messaging must change or risk being perceived by customers as unclear and disjointed.

Once High Beam began to identify the profit drivers that their Intelligent Monitor software could have an impact on, thanks to the National Products project, they were able to validate a number of their assumptions. Most of all, getting everyone on the same page and communicating the same message is critical to distinguishing one's company as profit-driven.

Communication

Once the executive team is on board and the management team knows their role in supporting a profit-centered go-to-market sales strategy, it is important to let the whole organization know that the company is all about winning in the marketplace. That means winning new customers, winning new deals, winning against competitors, winning greater margin, and ultimately winning with investors. Devising and pinning down a communications strategy is the best way to ensure that the right messages are communicated, that the employees understand that the changes are in support of the company's overall strategy, and that the program is aimed at making everyone more successful.

High Beam CEO Julie Moore asked her marketing communications team to put together an internal marketing campaign that would convey her vision and the executive team's commitment to becoming a profit-driven, customer-enabling machine. In doing so, she wanted to communicate a message to the entire company: "Whatever your role, we are all in business to serve the customer." When you can add that you are in business to help customers achieve their profit goals, that is a powerful message indeed.

As part of the communications campaign, Julie wanted to include executive overviews and scripts that would help them communicate the strategy. This included talking points and meeting agendas with topics, facts, and information that would bolster the approach. Most of all, she wanted every communication to include mention of the incredible success they had achieved at National Products. She was sure everyone had heard about it, but now she could put into context and use it as proof that High Beam was going in the right direction.

Execution and Accountability

Implement Training

As part of Julie's overall commitment to profit-centered selling she charged High Beam's EVP of sales, Ralph Morris, with identifying the competencies required to bring the entire sales team up to speed with the new selling strategy. She knew there would be those who would embrace it, those who would resist it, and those who would do their best. At the core of the process was building financial competency, because just about everything about selling profit improvement is tied to customer financials.

So financial education was the foundation. Also, they needed to operationalize their profit improvement process. This would need to include their newly acquired sales and marketing tools like the Business Analyzer, which helps salespeople understand customer financials and business issues. National Products was the perfect case study for learning and applying new skills that needed to be a part of the education program.

Deploy the Process

Using the tools and the training, it was now up to the sales leadership team to implement the new selling approach. It takes time, coaching, and ongoing feedback. High Beam established a coaching regimen that followed the Business Analyzer and Profit Analyzer process to ensure that all the salespeople were approaching their sales opportunities with profit improvement in mind, first and foremost. It also took help from marketing, sales support, and IT to ensure that salespeople had access to the customer information and resources they needed to build profit improvement proposals. The expectation was that sales managers should participate in the development and the presentation of profit improvement proposals to keep the organization learning and progressing.

Measurement

One of the things that Julie wanted to accomplish was to get a better reading on the sales pipeline: how the sales team was progressing in calling higher, identifying larger opportunities, and being able to position High Beam for new opportunities. Working with IT and sales operations, she asked if they could quantify the key metrics (including revenue growth, margin, opportunity costs, and deal profitability) as well as capture the profit impact delivered to customers. That would be the Holy Grail, being able to document within High Beam the total dollar amount of profit impact the company had produced for customers.

Julie had an ulterior motive for this. If there was a high degree of certainty, or even confirmation, that the company had delivered, say, $1 billion in profit improvement to their customers, that would be a very strong story for the Wall Street analysts that were hammering her on revenue growth and the company's competitive position in the market. But most of all, there needed to be an ROI on the profit-centered sales process, and the goals outlined earlier would serve to provide that.

One of the best ways to build a strong marketing story is to build a database of profit success stories, and also get customers to serve as case studies and to be willing to serve as references. That was part of Julie's vision for positioning High Beam as an industry-leading company.

Chapter 11

Why High Beam Industries Won—The Customer's View

"Opportunity does not knock,
it presents itself when you beat the down the door."
—*Kyle Chandler*

From *Factory Journal*, December issue, by Ken Woods, contributing editor:

Background: National Products recently announced an ambitious project to improve the quality of its enterprise-wide production. The company's CEO Harold Roth and CFO John Fuller sat for an interview with our managing editor, Ken Woods. Of particular interest were their reflections on how and why they awarded the project to High Beam Industries rather than a long-favored vendor with a 60% installed base.

MM: Let's start with the genesis of the project. Why did you begin researching production quality?

JF: It was the production team that brought it to our attention. They were experiencing assembly line shutdowns, weak throughput numbers, and higher-than-normal defect rates. And of course we knew our spray gun systems were aging, but we were trying to squeak by for a couple more years until our financial performance improved. But when we saw the numbers from our big-box customers, we saw how much it was hurting revenues. So we knew we needed to take action.

MM: So you talked to your spray gun vendors?

JF: We thought it was the spray guns, but first we wanted a better, more precise view of the problem and its causes. Our head of manufacturing commissioned an in-depth production quality improvement audit, and our Six Sigma team put a plan together to get started. The idea was to dedicate about three months to the effort, and pull the team together, have finance scrub the data, and, as a team, determine the best course of action. As much as we wanted to get any conversions finished before next spring's construction season, we also knew we wanted to get it just right.

HR: I personally asked the Six Sigma team to home in on the production monitoring reporting, I believed it was woefully short on data to help the entire team make good and timely decisions. I was eager to get the findings of the audit to better understand what was happening and what we could do about it. After all, it was a real sore spot, and we were being impacted every day. If it was something I could wave a magic wand at and get us a world-class production environment, I would. But magic wands cost money.

MM: Were the results of the audit what you expected?

JF: They were very thorough. They isolated the problems in a way that made us believe we could solve them without breaking the bank or disrupting our manufacturing process excessively. And yes, the main issue was the aging spray gun systems installed in 20 of our 42 plants. They were continually clogging, and you know how that snowballs: line interruptions, production slowdowns, throughput drops. Maintenance gets pulled into repairs so they can't do preventive work, and we're already lean there.

HR: Whenever I think of a maintenance guy working on a breakdown, I can't help wondering where the next breakdown will occur because he has to neglect the preventive work. I am reassured that's not happening, but I think that if we don't get these nagging problems solved, that would logically be the case.

MM: So the audit mainly uncovered productivity issues?

JF: No, there was another alarming discovery. Our defects were rising rapidly. So there was another chain reaction: defects required refinishing. Of course, your production cycle assumes some defects and refinishing, usually due to operator error on the part of new employees. But the audit uncovered defect rates well above normal. They also found that the aging guns were a lot less energy-efficient, so the over-spray and other factors posed environmental concerns. We want a safe workplace, and we want to maintain a good sustainability rating as a company.

HR: As for my interest in our having good production monitoring data available, the audit answered that. Our systems were old, having been partly developed internally and partly provided by a long-time vendor that helps us monitor maintenance. I was fairly certain we were operating without enough good data.

JF: Harold's right. I'm a finance guy but with a technology background and a strong interest in the decision support capabilities of all of our technology. A couple of years ago I drove our investment in a new enterprise resource planning (ERP) system. I put my neck on the line for that one, over $50 million dollars. But I also knew that as a company we were incredibly inefficient in our process management and decision support reporting.

MM: Shouldn't your ERP system be giving you great production-related data?

JF: Ideally yes. It does give us an integrated real-time view of core business processes. It tracks business resources—cash, raw materials, production capacity—and the status of business commitments: orders, purchase orders, and payroll. The applications that make up the system share data across the various departments. And even though I knew that we were plugging in all elements of our production process and facilities, I still believed we were not getting enough out of the system. That's because it was not designed for spray gun systems specifically. We needed to upgrade a system that would give us better data in real time.

HR: So you see, the focus of our quality initiative automatically expanded beyond the technical requirements of the spray gun systems themselves. We frankly needed better reporting just as much as we needed better guns.

MM: By the time you documented the project requirements, what outcomes were you looking for?

JF: We were ambitious, but not extravagantly so. We targeted increased product throughput of 5%, reduced defects/refinishing of 5%, reduced production downtime for maintenance and repairs at a healthy 10%. And we specified that we needed to see energy efficiencies meeting our corporate sustainability goals, and, of course, better monitoring and reporting.

MM: Now I believe you chose not to put out an RFP?

HR: That's right. At first we intended to, but then our manufacturing team, especially a number of the targeted plant managers, convinced us that the energy and resources required to document, publish, distribute, and then process all of those in-depth proposals would actually cost us more money than it was worth. They believed they were very close to the specifications and could discern the companies best suited to support us. So when asked about it, I supported the decision to narrow the list to the companies our team was comfortable with and not issue an RFP. So we ended up with a very short list of two: Quality Brands and High Beam Industries.

MM: From my information it's obvious why Quality Brands made the list. They had about 60 percent of your business and had long been urging you to upgrade with their guns. The reasons High Beam Industries was your other short-lister are less apparent.

JF: We weren't expecting High Beam to make our short list either, but when we gave their account manager a courtesy meeting, she surprised us by talking not just about spray guns and production matters but also about her company's software investment, which sounded like it might help us get more out of our own ERP, the way Harold and I were looking for.

MM: I see, so it came down to a software decision in High Beam's favor?

HR: Oh, no, not at all. The software she described was intriguing because it told us she knew what concerns we had here in the C-suite—not just the concerns on the production floor. She was looking at our quality initiative from the same view John and I have—not from a pure production point of view, and not just with an eye to selling us her spray gun systems.

MM: How did she do that—for example, after her initial suggestion in your courtesy meeting with her?

HR: John's going to have more to say about that than I do, but I will say it was the first time I had a salesperson start off a proposal with, "Here's how much we can improve your profits"—and then give a dollar figure. I've listened to some really talented and hard-working salespeople, and I pay attention when they tell me why their products are better than others, or how their company will give us better service, and I certainly pay attention when they make price concessions! But then it's still up to us to do the hard work of figuring out how their solutions will do what John and I have to think about all the time: improve our profits.

JF: Yes, if I had to net it out, I would say that High Beam's salesperson made it a business decision, not a technical decision. And furthermore, she made it a business decision based on profit, not the features of her product.

MM: I assume you mean figuratively, because it's not the salesperson's job to work up the financials?

JF: That's been true in the past, but I assure you that won't be true from now on for Harold and me. That's what I want to hear every time somebody asks for our business from now on. She really did dig deep into our financials. She looked at our trends, ratios, or revenue concerns, our rising costs, and the

Financials

pressure on our margins. Before she ever asked a single question about our production quality audit, she asked many about what we were trying to accomplish business-wise, financially speaking. She sounded like one of our board members! She even picked up on our concerns about managing capital with lower inventories and how they could impact that. That wasn't even in the requirements. She dug it out and was very persuasive on the subject.

HR: She also gave us a good education on the big-picture ERP story. John was pretty flattered when she referred to a speech he had given on the subject—she had found it on YouTube—now that's due diligence. So she knew what he was after. And she built on that

Education

by showing us how our ERP system should integrate with our

production system in ways that ran all the way through our entire supply chain. This was not something we had factored in. And, she didn't just tell us how her solution should fit in—she also had the big picture of how John and I look at it and what we need from it. She gave us a white paper with examples of other successes in similar environments, and we passed it around to the whole team.

JF: I don't think it's exaggerating to say that she also had a vision for our business. I mean, she looked well beyond the project requirements. Of course in that she had the advantage of her company, which had already invested in leading-edge maintenance monitoring software using the latest in wireless, cloud computing technologies. She shared her company's thought leadership around how spray gun systems and the software that provides intelligent monitoring of repairs, calibration, quality, and maintenance can all inform the ERP system. She saw that would give us timely decision support data so that we could implement solutions before small problems became big problems.

HR: It was also the way she presented her ROI. She didn't just take the operational data and show how being more productive or efficient would justify the costs. She translated the improvements into profitability. She took a corporate view and not just a project view when she presented and defended her profit improvement solution. We often have to sift through reams of technical data and pricing tables to figure out what our investment will be. Seldom do we see it both up front and then well defended using our financials and internal data.

JF: And we can't overlook one thing she hit hard that you often don't see even mentioned in sales presentations: accountability. I mean, before she even asked for the business, she laid out a plan for measuring the profit improvement we would achieve. She was frankly pretty assertive about our own obligations in measuring the results, and I couldn't argue with that. As a CFO, I am in a position, along with Harold, to allocate the right resources. We often don't know or think of all of the things that we should be doing as an organization to document the impact of many of our initiatives. Her plan made it straightforward for us to assign accountabilities and resources to ensure we get the return we are looking for.

It was a huge investment and not one we were planning. However, my philosophy is that we are here to make good decisions for our employees and shareholders, and being short-sighted was a bigger risk than going all in on the enterprise-wide retrofit.

HR: That's true. And as the guy who had to go to the board and get funding for a project that was supposed to be just a spray gun systems replacement and was now an enterprise-wide retrofit plus new monitoring software integrated with EFP, I sure appreciated the attention she gave to justifying the expenditure in board language, not the language of the production line.

MM: Thank you very much. I'd like to reconnect after your project is completed.

Chapter 12

It's a Mindset—10 Building Blocks to Becoming a Profit Hero

"It's never too late to be what you might have been."
—*George Eliot*

Carol Dweck writes in her book, *Mindset—The New Psychology of Success*, that there two distinct mindsets that define how people live and learn: a *fixed mindset* and a *growth mindset*. Having a *fixed mindset* means believing that your qualities are carved in stone. It causes you to feel the need to prove to yourself over and over again that you are talented and smart. It is about constantly validating yourself. You are consumed by the need to confirm your intelligence, character, or personality. In every situation you ask yourself, *Do I look smart? Will I succeed? Will I be accepted or rejected? Will I feel like a winner or a loser?*

Having a *growth mindset* means believing that where you are is the starting point. You believe that your unique qualities are things you can cultivate through your effort. Even though people have different talents, aptitudes, and interests, you believe that everyone can change and grow through application and experience. You can develop by stretching yourself to learn something new. People with a growth mindset don't just look for challenges, they thrive on them. Most view failure as a learning experience to be built on. You don't have to look any further than sports to see how a growth mindset plays out. Basketball great Michael Jordan sought out and even constructed his own personal challenges, which fueled his desire to learn and improve his game.

Being aware of these mindsets can be instructive in understanding how salespeople approach their profession. I have spent the past 20 years helping salespeople become stronger businesspeople and developing their knowledge and skills to become successful at profit-centered selling. I have experienced both mindsets up close. The biggest obstacle I encounter is resistance to change. Those with a fixed mindset tend to wait and see; they need proof and validation; they want to know that no matter what is changing, their success is achievable before they commit to doing things differently. Their resistance is expressed as *informed doubt based on experience.* In contrast, those with a growth mindset believe that mastering something new will help them become more successful, even if the end state is not assured.

Susan Stafford is a fictional character, the composite of many successful profit-centered salespeople I have known. Most have a growth mindset, and all are willing to stretch themselves to find the next level of success they can achieve. Susan was willing to learn and apply new ideas. She was not afraid to fail. She had a lofty vision to change the game by selling at the executive level and selling profit improvement in such a bold fashion. In doing so, she became a peer of the National Products decision makers in a way that will drive her success for years to come.

From Susan's experience—that is, the experience of all the real-world successful salespeople I have known—I have identified 10 building blocks that she and all Profit Heroes use in becoming elite salespersons. With these 10 building blocks, you too can become a Profit Hero to your customers and to your company.

1. Learn Finance

The single most important competency you need in profit-centered selling is financial literacy. Regardless of where you are on the finance curve, the more you learn about the economics of your customer's business the better prepared you will be to identify the core profit drivers that impact it. It is only then that you can begin to apply solutions that raise profits.

Financial literacy is also critical for knowing how to speak the language of the C-suite and understanding how they make economic decisions. Listen to your customer's earnings calls; use the language they use to align with their business. Doing so allows you to have high-level conversations that build your image as a strong businessperson. Executive decision makers want relationships with other businesspeople who understand their business and know how to impact it in ways they have yet to think of, or in ways they have yet to achieve. Create financial curiosity and stay hungry.

2. Brand Yourself

Building a professional brand communicates the unique knowledge, capabilities, and experiences that will help you differentiate yourself from your competition. Social networking has opened up new channels of communication, and there are now many ways to integrate tools like LinkedIn into your personal branding. Express a point of view; use a tagline that attracts attention; write an article; link articles and areas of interest or insightful books you have read to your online profile with a quick note on why they are important to customers. Letting your customers know how you are different and that you are a profit-centered business resource will build your image as a thought leader and a highly knowledgeable expert in your industry. Your brand strategy needs to include how, what, where, when, and to whom you plan on communicating and delivering on your unique messages. Make sure it's an authentic brand that you can deliver sincerely and consistently.

3. Elevate Your Game

No matter where you sell on the decision-making food chain, your goal should be to elevate. It is not easy getting to the C-suite. In the real world, the legacy of selling at the operational or functional level may prohibit immediate access to the executive levels. Educating, collaborating, and partnering with non-decision makers and influencers is how you elevate or reduce resistance and avert an administrative blockade. You need to have the mindset that no matter where you are in the organization, your goal is to elevate to those who directly manage profitability. For instance, plant managers own the profitability for their facility and make a lot of decisions locally. If you are able to leverage those relationships and collaborate to build operational support or validation of your profit improvement strategy, they can serve to provide you exposure to the highest levels. Profit Heroes know that, over time, doing business at the highest levels accelerates the sales process, increases the probability of success, reduces competitive exposure, and improves margins because decisions are based on return on investment and profitability.

4. Build an Executive Referral Network

Building a strong network of executive-level referral sources will accelerate your sales cycle, reduce competition, and bring new thought leadership to new executives, helping you create greater demand for your solutions. The challenge is how to get there. The competition to get into the C-suite is intense. It is difficult to get high-level executives to respond to solicitations if you don't know them. They will, however, respond to professional peers who make recommendations around ideas or solutions that might improve their business. Building and nurturing an executive referral network is hard work. But it is one of the top best practices Profit Heroes use to build business.

5. Think Big

Selling profit improvement enables you to think beyond just the immediate opportunity and to envision the longer-term impact you can have on the customer's business. Executives manage their business by looking ahead, seeing around the corner to anticipate trends and changes that will help them grow their business profitably. Susan Stafford recognized that competing for National Products' quality improvement project by itself was a losing proposition given her lack of relationships and the high level of penetration her competitor had. She didn't limit herself to thinking about a different way to compete for the existing scope of the project but instead thought big and redefined the scope of the opportunity by looking at it as financial decision and not a technical one. Thinking big starts with a vision of where you believe the relationship can go. Envision a perfect world in which the customer deploys every product and service you offer, and see the result. Thinking big starts with having the confidence that you can identify and quantify profit improvement that changes the customer's business.

6. Be Bold

Get outside of your comfort zone. Don't fear proposing solutions that change the way a customer is approaching a business problem or opportunity. Being bold means asking for information that may be closely held or "typically not provided." Being bold is asking for a meeting with a C-level executive, knowing that you or your company has not been there in the past. Being bold is communicating a strong point of view even when you know conventional wisdom is against you. Being bold is being willing to guarantee an outcome your competitor will not. Being bold is stating your desire and your ability to deliver profit improvement and then doing it.

7. Belong

Profit Heroes aspire to build peer relationships with economic decision makers. They are a special class of business partner that is viewed as an earnings contributor. A peer is someone who works every day to identify business challenges or areas of improvement that the customer should attend to. A peer develops new strategies to address the company's financial goals. Once an executive returns your call, invites you in, and provides you with an advanced view of a critical business need or issue, you know you have arrived; you know you belong.

8. Deliver

One of the biggest changes in business today is the new focus on financial accountability. That goes for suppliers as well. Gone are the days when you could throw around directional or anecdotal evidence and get away with it. Decision makers are looking for suppliers who deliver on their promises, and not just by delivering a service or solution, but by delivering on the economic impact they promised. Don't promise anything you can't deliver, and deliver everything you promise: That's never been more important.

9. Prove It

Proving that you can deliver, or have delivered, the profit improvement you promise is a team sport. Proving your impact actually starts before the sale. Establishing the guidelines and markers that measure and track results is the first step. Gaining the support and commitment of the economic decision maker must be done early in the process. You have to make a business case (with the help of millions of dollars of profit impact) that internal resources need to be allocated to track and measure the leading and lagging indicators of success. The most important point of proving profit improvement is ensuring that there is a mutual agreement with the customer on how to communicate and report that success. Every time you prove the financial impact you deliver you'll improve your leverage with executive-level decision makers and make the next project easier for them to invest in.

10. Believe

You have to believe in yourself first. Know that you can change the game for your customer and for your company. Know that if you invest the time to become a profit-centered salesperson and succeed in delivering profit improvement, you will differentiate yourself from 95% of all salespeople you compete with. Believe in your company; be confident that if they experience the profit improvement that comes with selling economic impact, they will also invest in you and your business. Finally, believe in your customers. Know that most will reward you for your innovation, perseverance, and commitment to improving their profitability.

Resource Center

Selling to Privately Held Companies

I am often asked about the challenges of finding financial and operational information on privately held companies. It is difficult, but it can be done. Of course, private companies are dealing with the same financial challenges that their competitors are—things like growing revenue, being operationally efficient, and using their capital effectively. Private companies do not have to report their financials, so it is difficult to know how well they are performing. But there are a few simple steps you can take to expand your knowledge before you engage an executive. I break it down into three areas: Industry Analysis, Competitive Analysis, and Company Analysis.

Industry Analysis

If I know an industry well, I will look for the most recent trends and changes affecting the companies I am pursuing. I have worked with healthcare for years, and the rate of change in that industry has accelerated tenfold because of the Affordable Care Act. Websites like Becker Hospital Review (www. beckershospitalreview.com) and Healthcare Finance News (www.healthcarefinancenews.com) provide daily updates on key events and changes in the industry. For example, I have found important information about the healthcare industry's growth strategies, which now focus on mergers and acquisitions. Executives talk about the unavoidable industry consolidation as the new healthcare law is fully implemented. They cover things like the challenge and implications of getting doctors on board in the value-based payment system. I have found in-depth articles on hospital supply chain efficiency trends. These websites, and many of those in other industries, are valuable resources with information that can provide you a strong backdrop to the issues that might resonate with executives.

Even if I don't know an industry well, I have found that some of the same resources can be instructive. Also, as I pointed out in Chapter 6, some public companies will provide industry information in their 10K reports. In their 2012 10K Form, for example, Community Health Systems, Inc., provided valuable information about the hospital industry and its structure (e.g., percent of resources devoted to acute care, rehabilitation, and psychiatric services), industry spending levels, and more. Also, McKinsey and other consulting companies provide free articles and white papers on a wide range of industries that can serve to educate you about key issues.

Competitive Analysis

If the company I'm researching has competitors that are publicly held, I find it very helpful to look at their financials. Hoovers. com and OneSource (subscription services) provide side-by-side comparisons of major competitors in terms of their sales, gross profit margin, net profit margins, return on assets, inventory turns, and days outstanding on receivables. The comparisons often include the industry and market medians for those key metrics.

By understanding the gross margins and other key metrics within an industry you can make educated guesses about the priorities or pressures a company is facing in trying to remain competitive in their market. For instance, if an industry has thin operating margins, you know that protecting price, managing cost of goods sold, speeding up inventory turns, and achieving greater operational efficiency will be very important. If a company operates in a high-margin industry, retaining customers and growing market share are probably huge issues.

I also go to a competitor's 10K report to understand the risk factors, which will be similar to those of a private company. If a public company includes industry overviews or talks about their strategies, you can learn a lot about what your private company is facing or trying to do in their market.

Company Analysis

The other challenge in researching private companies is finding and accessing key executives. I start with the company's website, where there is often good, in-depth information about the company, markets served, products and services, and key executives. I always look at their press releases to see who has been hired, fired, or promoted. Another resource is The Official Board (www. theofficialboard. com), which provides organizational structures, names, and emails; however, it charges a fee and doesn't always have data on privately held companies.

I have found Jigsaw (www.jigsaw. com, now www.data.com) to be a very valuable resource for researching private companies. It is a community data base that allows you to access targeted contact information. By contributing names (business card information) to the data base, you earn credits that you can use to research and find other names by company, function, level, title, and location. I have found the names of hundreds of contacts at private (and public) companies, including executives, division heads, and functional managers. When you find a potentially important contact, you can spend your points to get his or her address, phone, number, and email address.

LinkedIn (www.linkedin.com) has become a valuable resource as well. As I pointed out in discussing Susan Stafford's approach, using LinkedIn to find contacts and the people they are connected to can both identify potential targets and provide opportunities to gain referrals. You can also use LinkedIn's email service to contact them directly. Other websites that can be helpful include ZoomInfo (www.zoominfo.com) and Spoke (www.spoke.com).

Finally, it should go without saying that more well-known resources, like the major search engines (Google, Bing, and Yahoo), business journals, industry associations, and the business section of the local newspaper, can provide a treasure trove of information about companies and their key executives. These sources are not consistently useful; in some cases you will find a lot of valuable information and in other cases very little. Unfortunately, there aren't any shortcuts, but aggregating information from multiple sources can help you paint a picture of the company's growth and expense management profile and what might be changing in their company.

Asking the Right Questions

The information you are able to find about a private company can be a mixed bag. The most reliable research is always done face-to-face with the executive. Asking the right questions in the right way will garner the best information. If you have been able to learn about key industry trends, you might ask the executive how his company plans to implement its growth strategy given the challenges in the market. You might ask how the company is approaching expense management and if there are any key initiatives or strategies in place to address their need to become more efficient. And, you might ask what plans they have to expand or invest capital into their operation. Following Susan Stafford's lead and elevating the conversation to one about profitability will ensure that you are able to get the executive interested in investing time and sharing more information.

Useful Websites for Customer Discovery, Analysis, and Thought Leadership

The following websites can be useful resources for supporting customer research and identifying industry trends and thought leadership.

Ask.com—www.ask.com
Helpful website for asking questions about business and finance

Becker Hospital Review—www.beckershospitalreview.com
Provides healthcare-related information about current events, executive changes and information, as well as links to other industry-related resources.

Chief Financial Officer—www.cfo.com
A resource for articles, white papers, and general financial information.

Chief Executive Officer—www.ceo.com
A website dedicated to CEOs. Provides great content, thought leadership, and news. Includes videos and CEO Watch to follow CEOs' professional moves.

Chief Information Officer—www.cio.com
News, analysis, blogs, and videos on the latest trends in information technology. Includes white papers, research, and hosts the CIO Executive Council, which is a global community dedicated to technology.

Chief Technology Officer—www.cto.org
News and resources covering the technology market

Chief Marketing Officer—www.cmo.com
A website dedicated to marketing related trends and issues

CNN Money—www.cnnmoney.com
Business news and current events

eHow—www.ehow.com/ehow-money
Helpful website for asking questions about business, financial ratios, and more

Forbes Magazine—www.forbes.com
Business magazine

Fox Business News—www.foxbusiness.com
Business news and current events

Google—www.google.com
A valuable source for researching companies, people, industries, markets, and articles.

Healthcare Finance News—www.healthcarefinancenews.com
Provides information about current trends in the healthcare industry, including the latest on the Affordable Care Act and its implications. Also a source for white papers and other thought leadership resources.

Hoovers—www.hoovers.com
Subscription website with access to Dun & Bradstreet data base of company information. Also includes industry overviews and other useful information.

Inc. Magazine—www.inc.com
Articles and industry trends. A great resource for researching privately held companies.

Investopedia — www.investopedia. c o m / w a l k t h r o u g h / corporate-finance/
The complete guide to corporate finance. A resource for learning about business finance.

Jigsaw—www.jigsaw (now data.com) www.jigsaw.com Community data base that allows the user to build credits for accessing target contact information. You can find names by company, function, level, title, and location.

McKinsey—www.mckinsey.com
Comprehensive thought leadership and information by industry, function, and region. An excellent resource for company information, trends, and the latest thinking on business issues.

The Official Board—www.theofficialboard.com
Organizational charts of the companies making over 100 million in revenue. For a fee, you can also get connected with key executives. Great networking and business intelligence tool.

OneSource—www.onesource.com
Provides business information solutions around company, executive, and industry intelligence.

Selling Power—www.sellingpower.com
Resource for salespeople and sales leadership. Includes blogs, white papers, webinars, newsletters, and more on the latest trends in selling.

Spoke—center.spoke.com
A personal directory service (and contact sourcing data base) that enables you to leverage personal contacts and find new leads.

PriceWaterhouseCoopers—www.pwc.com

A resource for thought leadership and information by industry. An excellent resource for researching companies, trends, and the latest thinking on business-related issues.

Seeking Alpha—http://seekingalpha.com
Business and financial information on publicly held companies from an investor's perspective.

Supply Chain Brain—www.supplychainbrain.com
Supply chain–dedicated website with over 70 categories of supply chain management–related topics. Includes videos, blogs, white papers, research, and a supplier directory.

Wall Street Journal—www.wsj.com
Covers economic and international business topics and financial news.

Yahoo Finance—http://finance.yahoo.com
Comprehensive financial website with market news, trends, and company financials.

Yahoo Finance Conference Call Calendar—http://biz.yahoo.com/cc/ Yahoo Finance Earning Call Calendar provides a daily list of companies conducting an earnings call; you can access the call directly from this website.

YouTube—www.youtube.com
A great research tool for finding corporate and individual presentations and interviews.

ZoomInfo—www.zoominfo.com
A comprehensive source of business information. Information is gathered from the same publicly available web sources that are searched by other major search engines (such as Yahoo and Google) and are accessible to any person surfing the web.

About the Author

Bob Rickert, CEO of PCS Strategies, has counseled some of the country's top enterprises on how to dramatically accelerate profit-centered selling, helping executives transform their businesses from product- and price-driven organizations to market leaders focused on delivering hard-dollar profit impact for their customers. His clients have realized sustainable profit growth by better aligning their core sales and financial competencies, marketing messages, and go-to-market strategies with the ever-changing market complexities. He brings a unique vantage point from his work with CEOs on strategy, CFOs on deploying financial disciplines, HR directors on corporate culture, and sales leadership on going to market in a differentiated way. His clients include industry leaders in manufacturing, healthcare, logistics, banking, energy, and industrial distribution. He is also a contributing author to two books on sales force development and has published numerous articles and white papers. He lives in Chicago. Contact Bob Rickert at (847) 971-8259; bob@pcsstrategies.com.